Leon Trotsky

THE PERMANENT REVOLUTION

Translated by
Max Shachtman

Gutenberg Publishers
2011

Gutenberg Publishers
Kapaau, Hawaii

gutenbergpublishers@gmail.com

Copyright @ Gutenberg Publishers, 2011

Gutenberg Publishers, as our name suggests, is
committed to the preservation of the printed word.
Each reprint we publish is carefully prepared,
cleaned, and preserved, producing an accurate
facsimile of the original edition.

ISBN 978-1-61427-997-6

Leon Trotsky

THE PERMANENT REVOLUTION

Translated by
Max Shachtman

℘

PIONEER PUBLISHERS
NEW YORK, 1931

PRINTED BY THE MILITANT PRESS IN MAY, 1931

Table of Contents

Preface to the American Edition

As this book goes to press in the English language, the whole thinking part of the international working class, and in a sense, the whole of "civilized" humanity, listens with particularly keen interest to the reverberations of the economic turn taking place on the major part of the former czarist empire. The greatest attention in this connection is aroused by the problem of collectivizing the peasant holdings. And no wonder: in this sphere the break with the past assumes a particularly clear-cut character. But a correct evaluation of collectivization is unthinkable without a general conception of the socialist revolution. And here on an even higher plane, we are again convinced that everything in the field of Marxian theory is bound up with practical activity. The most remote, and it would seem, "abstract" disagreements, if they are thought out to the end, will sooner or later be expressed in practise, and the latter allows not a single theoretical mistake to be made with impunity.

The collectivization of peasant holdings is, it is understood, the most necessary and fundamental part of the socialist transformation of society. The volume and tempo of collectivization, however, are not only determined by the government's will, but, in the final analysis, by the economic factors: by the height of the country's economic level, the relationship between industry and agriculture and consequently by the technical resources of agriculture itself.

Industrialization is the motive force of the whole newer culture and, by that, the only conceivable basis of socialism. In the conditions of the Soviet Union, industrialization means first of all the strengthening of the base of the proletariat as a ruling class. Simultaneously, it creates the material and technical premises for the collectivization of agriculture. The tempos of both these processes are interdependent. The proletariat is interested in the highest tempos for these processes, in so far as the new society that is to be created is thus best protected from external danger, and at the same time creates a source for systematically improving the material level of the toiling masses.

However, the tempo that can be accomplished is limited by the whole material and cultural position of the country, by the mutual relationship between the city and village and by the most urgent needs of the masses, who can sacrifice their today for the sake of tomorrow *only up to a certain point*. The best and most advantageous tempos are those which not only produce the most rapid development of industry and collectivization at the given moment, but secure the necessary resistance of the social régime, that is, first of all the strengthening of the alliance of the workers and peasants, which alone prepares the possibility of further successes.

From this point of view, the general historical criterion by which the party and state leadership directs the development of industry as planned economy assumes decisive significance. Here two principle variants are possible: (a) the course described above towards the economic entrenchment of the proletarian dictatorship in one country until further victories of the international proletarian revolution (the viewpoint of the Left Opposition); (b) the course towards the construction of an isolated national socialist society and at that "in the shortest historical time" (the present official viewpoint).

These are two distinct, and in the final analysis, directly opposed theoretical conceptions of socialism. Out of these flow basically different strategy and tactics.

In the limits of this foreword we cannot consider anew the question of the construction of socialism in one country. Other of our works are devoted to this, particularly *The Criticism of the Draft Program of the Comintern**. Here we limit ourselves to the fundamental elements of the question. Let us recall, first of all, that the theory of socialism in one country was first formulated by Stalin in the fall of 1924, in complete contradiction not only to all the traditions of Marxism and the school of Lenin, but even to what Stalin wrote in the spring of the same year. From the standpoint of principle, the departure from Marxism by the Stalinist "school" in the question of socialist construction is no less significant than, for example, the break of the German social democracy with Marxism in the question of war and patriotism, in the fall of 1914, that is, exactly ten years before the Stalinist turn. This comparison has no accidental character. Stalin's "mistake", as well as the "mistake" of the German social democracy, is *national socialism*.

Marxism proceeds from world economy, not as a sum of national parts, but as a mighty, independent reality, which is created by the international division

*Published in 1929 by The Militant.

ix

of labor and the world market, and, in the present epoch, predominates over the national markets. The productive forces of capitalist society have long ago grown beyond the national frontier. The imperialist war was an expression of this fact. In the productive-technical respect, socialist society must represent a higher stage compared to capitalism. To aim at the construction of a *nationally isolated* socialist society means, in spite of all temporary successes, to pull the productive forces backward even as compared to capitalism. To attempt, regardless of the geographic, cultural and historical conditions of the country's development, which constitutes a part of the world whole, to realize a fenced-in proportionality of all the branches of economy within national limits, means to pursue a reactionary utopia. If the heralds and supporters of this theory nevertheless participate in the international revolutionary struggle (with what success is a different question) it is because as hopeless eclectics, they mechanically combine abstract internationalism with reactionary utopian national socialism. The consummate expression of this eclecticism is the program of the Comintern adopted by the Sixth Congress.

To expose completely one of the main theoretical mistakes, lying at the base of the national socialist conception, we can do nothing better than to quote the recently published speech of Stalin, devoted to the internal questions of American Communism.* "It would be wrong," says Stalin against one of the American factions, "not to take into consideration the

* This speech was delivered on May 6, 1929, was first published at the beginning of 1930, and under such circumstances that it acquires a "programmatic" significance.

specific peculiarities of American capitalism. The Communist party must consider them in its work. But it would be still more wrong to base the activity of the Communist party on these specific features, for the foundation of the activity of every Communist party, the American included, on which it must base itself, are the *general features* of capitalism, which are essentially the *same for all countries*, but not the specific features of *one* country. *It is precisely on this that the internationalism of the Communist parties rests.* The specific features are merely *supplementary* to the general features." (BOLSHEVIK, No. 1, 1930, page 8. Our emphasis.)

These lines leave nothing to be desired in the way of clarity. Under the guise of an economic motivation for internationalism, Stalin in reality presents a motivation for national socialism. It is false that world economy is simply a sum of similar national parts. It is false that the specific features are *"merely supplementary* to the general features", like warts on the face. In reality, the national peculiarities are a unique combination of the basic features of the world process. This originality can be of decisive significance for revolutionary strategy for a number of years. It is sufficient to recall the fact that the proletariat of a backward country has come to power many years before the proletariat of the advanced countries. This historic lesson alone shows that in spite of Stalin, it is absolutely wrong to base the activity of the Communist parties on some "general features", that is, on an abstract type of national capitalism. It is radically wrong to contend that this is what the "internationalism of the Communist parties rests upon". In reality, it rests on the inconsistency of a national state, which has long ago outlived itself and acts as a brake on the development of the productive forces. National capitalism cannot be conceived of, let alone reconstructed, except as a part of world economy.

The economic peculiarities of different countries are in no way of a subordinate character: It is enough to compare England and India, the United States and Brazil. But the specific features of national economy, no matter how great, enter as component parts, and in increaing measure into the higher reality, which is called world economy, and on which alone, in the final analysis, the internationalism of the Communist parties rests.

Stalin's characterization of the national peculiarities as a simple "supplement" to the general type, is in crying and yet not accidental contradiction to Stalin's understanding (that is, his lack of understanding) of the law of the uneven development of capitalism. This law, as is known, is proclaimed by Stalin as the most fundamental, most important and universal. With the help of the law of uneven development, which he has converted into an abstraction, Stalin attempts to solve all the riddles of existence. But it is astounding: He does not notice that *national peculiarity is the most general product of unevenness of historical development, its final result, so to say.* It is only necessary to understand this unevenness correctly, to consider it to its full extent, and also to extend it to the pre-capitalist past. A faster or slower development of productive forces; the expanded, or on the contrary, the contracted character of whole historical epochs—for example, of the middle ages, the guild system, enlightened absolutism, parliamentarism; the uneven development of the different branches of economy, different classes, different social institutions, different fields of culture—all these lie at the base of these na-tional "peculiarities". Originality of a national social type is the crystallization of the unevenness of its formation. The October revolution is the grandest manifestation of the unevenness of the historic process. The theory of the permanent revolution, which gave the *prognosis* of the October overthrow, supported it-self, by that alone, on the law of uneven historical de-velopment, not in its abstract form, but in the material crystallization of the social and political peculiarity of Russia.

Stalin resorted to the law of uneven development not in order to foresee in time the seizure of power by the proletariat of a backward country, but in order, af-ter the fact, in 1924, to foist upon the already vic-torious proletariat the task of constructing a national socialist society. But it is preciseiy here that the law of uneven development has nothing to do with the mat-ter, for it does not replace nor does it abolish the laws of world economy; on the contrary, it is subordinated to them.

By making a fetish of the law of uneven develop-ment, Stalin proclaims it a sufficient basis for national socialism, not as a type, common to all countries, but exceptional, Messianic, purely Russian. To construct an independent socialist society is possible, according to Stalin, only in Russia. By this alone he raises the national peculiarities of Russia not only above the "general features" of every capitalist nation, but also above world economy as a whole. This is just where the fatal flaw begins in the whole Stalin conception. The peculiarity of the U. S. S. R. is so immense that it makes possible the construction of its own socialism within its limits, regardless of what happens with the rest of humanity. As for other countries to which the

Messianic seal has not been affixed, their peculiarities are only "supplementary" to the general features, only a wart on the face. "It would be wrong", Stalin teaches, "to base the activities of the Communist parties on these specific features." This moral holds good for the American Communist Party, the British, South African and Serbian, but . . . not for the Russian, whose activity is based not on the "general features" but precisely on the "peculiarities". From this flows the thoroughly discordant strategy of the Comintern: while the U. S. S. R. "liquidates the classes" and builds national socialism, the proletariat of all the other countries, completely independent of actual national conditions, is obligated to uniform action according to the calendar (First of August, March Sixth, etc.). Messianic nationalism is complemented by bureaucratically abstract internationalism. This discordance runs through the whole program of the Comintern, and deprives it of any principled significance.

If we take England and India as the opposite poles of capitalist types, we must state that the internationalism of the British and Indian proletariat does not at all rest on the *similarity* of conditions, tasks and methods, but on their inseparable *interdependence*. The successes of the liberation movement in Inda presuppose a revolutionary movement in England, and the other way around. Neither in India, nor in England is it possible to construct an independent socialist society. Both of them will have to enter as parts into a higher entity. In this and only in this rests the unshakable foundation of Marxian internationalism.

Only recently, on March 8, 1930, PRAVDA expounded Stalin's unhappy theory anew, in the sense that "socialism, as a social-economic formation", that is, as a definite form of productive relations, can be absolutely realized "on the national scale of the U. S. S. R.". "The *complete victory of socialism* in the sense of a guarantee against the intervention of capitalist encirelement", is quite another matter—such a complete victory of socialism "actually demands the triumph of the proletarian revolution in several advanced countries". What abysmal decline of theoretical thought was required for such sorry scholasticism to be expounded in a learned guise on the pages of the central organ of Lenin's party! If we should assume for a minute the possibility of realizing socialism as a finished social system in the isolated framework of the U. S. S. R., then what would be the "complete victory" —what intervention could even be talked of then? The socialist order of society presupposes high levels of technique, culture and solidarity of the population. Since the U. S. S. R., at the moment of complete construction of socialism, will have, it must be assumed, a population of from 200,000,000 to 250,000,000, then we ask: What intervention could be talked of then? What capitalist country, or coalition of countries would dare think of intervention under these circumstances? The only conceivable intervention could be on the part of the U. S. S. R. But would it be needed? Hardly. The example of a backward country, which, in the course of several "five year plans" constructed a mighty socialist society with its own forces would mean a death blow to world capitalism, and would reduce to a minimum, if not to zero, the costs of the world proletarian revolution. This is why the whole Stalinist conception actually leads to the liquidation of the Communist International. And really, what could its historical significance be, if the fate of socialism is to be decided in the last resort . . . by the Gosplan [State Planning Commission] of the U. S. S. R.? In such a case, the task of the Comintern, along with the illustrious "Friends of the Soviet Union", would be to protect the construction of socialism from intervention, that is, in essence, to play the rôle of a frontier guard.

The article already mentioned above attempts to strengthen the correctness of the Stalinist conception with the very newest economic arguments: " . . . precisely now," PRAVDA says, "when productive relations on a socialist basis take deeper root not only in industry but also in agriculture, through the growth of the Soviet farms, through the gigantic rise in quantity and quality of the collective farms movement and the liquidation of the kulak as a class on the basis of complete collectivization, it shows more clearly the sorry bankruptcy of Trotsky-Zinoviev defeatism, which has meant in essence 'the Menshevik denial of the legitimacy of the October revolution' (Stalin)." (PRAVDA, March 8, 1930.)

These lines are really remarkable, and not merely for their glib tone which covers the complete confusion of thought. Together with Stalin, the author of the PRAVDA article accuses the "Trotskyist" conception of "denying the legitimacy of the October revolution". But it was precisely on the basis of this conception, that is, of theory of the permanent revolution, that the writer of these lines *foretold the inevitability* of the October revolution, thirteen years before it took place. And Stalin? Even after the February revolution, that is, from seven to eight months prior to the October overthrow, he came forward as a vulgar revolutionary democrat. It was necessary for Lenin to arrive in Petrograd (April 3, 1917) with his merciless struggle and ridicule of the conceited "old Bolsheviks" for Stalin carefully and unostentatiously to glide over from the democratic to the socialist position. This inner "regrowth" of Stalin, which by the way was never completed, took place, at any rate, not earlier than twelve years after the "legitimacy" of the seizure of power by the working class of Russia, before the beginning of the proletarian revolution in the West had been indicated.

But, in elaborating the theoretical prognosis of the October revolution, we did not at all believe that, by conquering state power, the Russian proletariat would exclude the former czarist empire from the sphere of world economy. We Marxists know the rôle and significance of state power. It is not at all a passive reflection of economic processes, as the social democratic servants of the bourgeois state fatalistically describe it. Power can have a gigantic significance, reactionary, as well as progressive, depending upon which class holds it in its hands. But the state power is nevertheless a weapon of superstructural order. The passing of power from the hands of czarism and the bourgeoisie into the hands of the proletariat, abolishes neither the processes, nor the laws of world economy. It is true that for a certain time after the October revolution, the economic ties between the Soviet Union and the world market were weakened. But it would be a monstrous mistake to generalize a phenomenon which was merely a short stage in the dialectical process. The international division of labor and the supra-national character of modern productive forces, not only retain, but will increase twofold and tenfold their significance for the Soviet Union, depending upon the degree of its economic ascent.

Every backward country that has become a part of capitalism has gone through various stages of decreasing or increasing dependence upon the other capitalist countries, but in general the tendency of capitalist development leads towards a collossal growth of world ties, which is expressed in the growth of foreign trade, including, of course, capital export as well. The dependence of England upon India naturally bears a qualitatively different character than the dependence of India upon England. But this difference is basically determined by the difference in the degree of development of their productive forces and not at all by the degree of their economic self-sufficiency. India is a colony, England—a metropolis. But if England were subjected today to an economic blockade, it would perish sooner than India. This, by the way, is one of the most convincing illustrations of the reality of world economy.

Capitalist development—not in the abstract formulæ of the second volume of *Capital*, which retain all their significance *as a stage in analysis*, but in historic reality—took place and could only take place by the systematic expansion of its base. In the process of its development, and consequently in the struggle with its internal contradictions, every national capitalism turns in ever increasing measure to the reserves of the "external market", that is, of world economy. The uncontrollable expansion growing out of the permanent internal crisis of capitalism, constitutes its progressive force until it becomes fatal.

The October revolution inherited from old Russia, besides the internal contradictions of capitalism, no less profound contradictions between capitalism as a whole and the pre-capitalist forms of production. These contradictions had and still have, a material character, that is, they are contained in the material relations between the city and country in definite proportions or disproportions of various branches of industry and national economy in general, etc. Some of the roots of these contradictions lie directly in the geographic and demographic conditions of the country, that is, they are nurtured by the surplus or the shortage of one or the other natural resource, and the historically created distribution of the masses of the people, etc. The strength of Soviet economy lies in the nationalization of the means of production and in their planned direction. The weakness of Soviet economy, on the other hand, besides the backwardness inherited from the past, lies in its present post-revolutionary isolation, that is, in its inability to gain access to the resources of world economy, not only on a socialist but even on a capitalist basis, that is, in the form of normal international credits, and "financing" in general, which plays such a decisive rôle for backward countries. However, the contradictions of its capitalist and pre-capitalist past not only do not disappear of themselves, but on the contrary, rise out of the twilight of the years of decline and destruction, revive and are accentuated simultaneously with the growth of Soviet economy, and in order to be overcome or even mitigated, demand at every step contact with the resources of the world market.

To understand what is happening now in the vast territory which the October revolution awakened to new life, we must always clearly picture to ourselves that to the old contradictions recently revived by the economic successes, there has been added a new and enormous contradiction between the concentrated character of Soviet industry, which opens up the possibility of an unprecedented tempo of development, and the isolation of Soviet economy, which excludes the possibility of a normal utilization of the reserves of world economy. The new contradiction, bearing down upon the old ones, leads to the fact that alongside of the exceptional successes, painful difficulties arise. The latter find their most immediate and strongest expression, felt daily by every worker and peasant, in the fact that the conditions of the toiling masses do not keep step with the general rise of economy, but even grow worse at present as a result of the food difficulties. The sharp crises of Soviet economy are a reminder that the productive forces created by capitalism are not adapted to a national framework and can be socialistically coordinated and harmonized only on an international scale. In other words, the crises of Soviet economy are not merely the maladies of growth, a sort of infantile sickness, but something immeasurably more significant—precisely that severe check of the world market, the very one "to which," in Lenin's words, "we are subordinated, with which we are bound up, and from which we cannot escape" (at the Eleventh Congress of the party, March 27, 1922).

From this, however, there in no way follows the denial of the historical "legitimacy" of the October revolution, a conclusion which smells of shameful philistinism. The seizure of power by the international proletariat cannot be a single, simultaneous act. The political superstructure—and a revolution is part of "superstructure"—has its own dialectic, which peremptorily interrupts the process of world economy, but does not abolish its deep-seated laws. The October revolution is "legitimate" as *the first stage in the world revolution*, which inevitably extends over decades. The interval between the first and the second stage has turned out to be considerably longer than we had expected. Nevertheless, it remains an interval, without being converted into an epoch of the self-sufficient construction of a national socialist society.

Out of the two conceptions of the revolution have come two principal lines on economic questions. The first rapid economic successes, which were completely unexpected by him, inspired Stalin in the fall of 1924 with the theory of socialism in one country as the culmination of a practical perspective for an isolated national economy. It was precisely in this period that Bucharin advanced his famous formula that in fencing ourselves off from world economy by the monopoly of foreign trade, we would be in a position to build up socialism "even at a snail's pace". This was the common formula of the bloc of the Centrists [Stalin] with the Rights [Bucharin]. Already at that time, Stalin tirelessly propounded the idea that the tempo of our industrialization is our "own affair", having no relation to world economy. Such a national self-contentment, however, could not last long, for it reflected the first, very brief stage of economic revival, which inevitably revived our dependence upon the world market. The first shocks of intra-state dependence, unexpected by the national socialists, created an alarm, which in the next stage turned into panic. To gain economic "independence" speedily with the aid of the fastest possible tempos of industrialization and collectivization!—this is the transformation that has taken place in the economic policy of national socialism in the past two years. Crawling was replaced all along the line by adventurism. The theoretical base under both is the same: a national socialist conception.

The basic difficulties, as was shown above, result from the objective situation, primarily from the isolation of the Soviet Union. We shall not stop here to consider to what degree this objective situation is itself a result of the subjective mistakes of the leadership (the false policy in Germany in 1923, in Bulgaria and Esthonia in 1924, in England and Poland in 1926, in China in 1925-1927; the present false strategy of the "third period", etc., etc.). But the sharpest convulsions in the U. S. S. R. are created by the fact that the present leadership tries to make a virtue out of a necessity, and out of the political isolation of the workers' state, constructs a program of an economically isolated socialist society. From this has resulted the attempt at complete socialist collectivization of peasant holdings on the basis of the pre-capitalist inventory—a most dangerous adventure which threatens to undermine the very possibility of collaboration between the proletariat and the peasantry.

And it is remarkable: just at the moment when this began to appear in all its sharpness, Bucharin, yesterday's theoretician of the "snail's pace" composed a pathetic hymn to the present "mad gallop" of industrialization and collectivization. It is to be feared that this hymn will soon be declared the greatest heresy. For there are already new melodies in the air. Under the influence of the resistance of economic reality, Stalin has been compelled to beat a retreat. Now the danger is that the adventurous offensive dictated by the panic of yesterday will turn into a panic-stricken retreat. Such an alternation of stages results inevitably from the nature of national socialism.

A realistic program of an isolated workers' state cannot set itself the aim of achieving "independence" from world economy, much less of constructing a national socialist society in the "shortest time". The task is not to accomplish the abstract maximum, but the most favorable tempo under the circumstances, that is, those that flow from internal and world economic conditions, strengthen the positions of the proletariat, prepare the *national elements* of the future international socialist society, and at the same time, and above all, systematically improve the living level of the proletariat, strengthening its union with the non-exploiting masses of the village. This perspective remains in force for the whole preparatory period, that is, until the victorious revolution in the advanced countries liberates the Soviet Union out of its present isolated position.

Some of the thoughts expressed here are developed in greater detail in other works of the author, particularly in the *Draft Program of the Comintern: A Criticism of Fundamentals*. In the near future we hope to publish a pamphlet especially devoted to an evaluation of the present state of economic development in the U. S. S. R. To these works, we are obliged to direct the reader who seeks a closer acquaintance with the way in which the problems of the permanent revolution are posed today. But the considerations brought out above are sufficient, let us hope, to reveal the whole significance of the struggle of principles that was carried on in recent years, and is carried on now in the form of contrasting two theories: *socialism in one country* and the *permanent revolution*. Only this timely significance of the question justifies the fact that we present here to foreign readers a book which is largely devoted to a critical re-establishment of the pre-revolutionary prognoses and theoretical disputes among the Russian Marxists. We could, of course, have selected a different form of expounding the questions that interest us. But this form was never created by the author, and was not selected by him of his own accord. It was imposed upon him partly by opponents and partly by the very course of political development. Even the truths of mathematics, the most abstract of the sciences, can best of all be learned in connection with the history of their discovery. This applies even more to the more concrete, that is, to the historically conditioned truths of Marxist policy. The history of the origin and development of the prognoses of the revolution in the conditions of pre-revolutionary Russia will, we think, bring the reader much closer and far more concretely to the essence of the revolutionary tasks of the world proletariat than a sophomoric and pedantic exposition of these political ideas, torn out of the conditions of struggle which gave birth to them.

March 29, 1930   L. Trotsky

Introduction

The present book is dedicated to the question which is intimately linked with the history of the three Russian revolutions. But not with that alone. This question has played an enormous rôle in recent years in the internal struggle of the C. P. S. U., it was carried into the C. I., played a decisive rôle in the development of the Chinese revolution and determined a whole series of most important decisions which are bound up with the revolutionary struggle of the countries of the East. It concerns the theory of the "permanent revolution" which, after the teaching of the epigones of Leninism (Zinoviev, Stalin, Bucharin, etc.) represents the original sin of "Trotskyism".

The question of the permanent revolution was once more raised in 1924 after a long interval, apparently quite unexpectedly. Political grounds for it, there were none: for it was a question of differences of opinion which long ago belonged to the past. Psychological grounds, on the contrary, there were many. The group of socalled "old Bolsheviks" which had opened up the fight against me, first of all counterposed this title to me. But a great obstacle in the path of this group was the year 1917. Important as had been the preceding history of ideological struggle and of preparation with regard to the party as a whole, as well as with regard to single individuals, this period found its highest and irrevocable test in the October revolution. *Not a single one of the epigones stood up under this test.* Without exception, they all adopted the vulgar position of the democratic Left wingers at the time of the February 1917 revolution. Not a single one of them raised the slogan of the struggle of the proletariat for power. They all regarded the course towards a socialist revolution as absurd or—still worse —as "Trotskyism". In this spirit they directed the party up till the arrival of Lenin from abroad and up till the appearance of his famous theses of April 4. Thereafter Kamenev endeavored, already in direct struggle against Lenin, openly to form a democratic wing of Bolshevism. Later, he was joined by Zinoviev, who had arrived with Lenin. Stalin, heavily compromised by his social patriotic position, stepped aside. He let the party forget his miserable articles and speeches of the decisive March weeks and gradually edged over to Lenin's standpoint. That is why the question rose by itself, so to speak: What did Leninism give to any one of these leading "old Bolsheviks" when *not a single one* of them showed himself capable of applying independently the theoretical and practical experiences of the party at the most important and most responsible historical moment? Attention had to be diverted from this question at all costs and another question substituted for it. To this end, it was decided to open fire on the permanent revolution. My adversaries did not, of course, foresee that by the creation of an artificial axis of struggle they would be compelled, without noticing it, to revolve around it themselves and manufacture a new world outlook for themselves.

In its essential features, the theory of the permanent revolution was formulated by me even before the
decisive events of 1905. Russia was approaching the
bourgeois revolution. Nobody in the ranks of the Russian social democracy (we all called ourselves social
democrats then) had any doubts that we were approaching a *bourgeois revolution*, that is, a revolution
produced by the contradictions between the development of the productive forces of capitalist society and
the outlived caste and state relationships of the
period of serfdom and the Middle Ages. In the struggle against the Narodniki and the anarchists, I had to
devote not a few speeches and articles in those days to
the Marxian analysis of the bourgeois character of
the impending revolution.

The bourgeois character of the revolution could not,
however, answer in advance the question as to which
classes would solve the tasks of the democratic revolution and what the mutual relations of these classes
would be. It was precisely at this point that the
fundamental strategical problems began.

Plechanov, Axelrod, Zasulitch, Martov, and following them, all the Russian Mensheviks, took as their
premise that to the liberal bourgeoisie, as the natural
claimant for power, belonged the leading rôle in the
bourgeois revolution. According to this schema, there
was assigned to the party of the proletariat the rôle
of the Left wing of the democratic front. The social
democracy was to support the liberal bourgeoisie
against the reaction and at the same time to defend
the interests of the proletariat against the liberal bourgeoisie. In other words, the Mensheviks understood
the bourgeois revolution principally as a liberal-con-
stitutional form.

Lenin posed the question differently. The liberation of the productive forces of bourgeois society from the fetters of serfdom signified for Lenin primarily a radical solution of the agrarian question in the sense of the complete liquidation of the landowning class and the revolutionary re-distribution of land ownership. Inseparably connected with this, was the destruction of the monarchy. Lenin set to work on the agrarian problem, which affected the life interests of the overwhelming majority of the population and at the same time constituted the basic problem of the capitalist market, with a truly revolutionary boldness. Since the liberal bourgeoisie, which confronts the workers as an enemy, is intimately bound by innumerable ties to large land ownership, the genuine democratic liberation of the peasantry can only be realized by the revolutionary cooperation of the workers and peasants. Their joint uprising against the old society, must, according to Lenin, in case of victory, lead to the establishment of the "democratic dictatorship of the proletariat and peasantry".

This formula is now repeated in the Communist International as a sort of supra-historical dogma, without the attempt at an analysis of the living historical experiences of the last quarter of a century, as though we had not been witnesses and participants in the revolution of 1905, the February revolution of 1917, and finally of the October overturn. Such an historical analysis, however, is all the more necessary because there never has been in history a régime of the "democratic dictatorship of the proletariat and peasantry".

In 1905, it was a question with Lenin of a strategical hypothesis which required a test in the reality of the class struggle. The formula of the democratic dictatorship of the proletariat and peasantry in large measure bore an intentionally algebraic* character. Lenin did not answer in advance the question of what the political relations would be between the two participants in the proposed democratic dictatorship, that is, of the proletariat and the peasantry. He did not exclude the possibility that the peasantry would be represented in the revolution by an independent party, independent in the double sense: that is, not only with regard to the bourgeoisie but also with regard to the proletariat, and at the same time, capable of realizing the democratic revolution in alliance with the party of the proletariat in struggle against the liberal bourgeoisie. Lenin even reckoned, as we shall soon see, with the possibility that the revolutionary peasants' party might constitute the majority in the government of the democratic dictatorship.

In the question of the decisive significance of the agrarian revolution for the fate of our bourgeois revolution, I was, at least since the autumn of 1902, that is, from the moment of my first flight abroad, a pupil of Lenin. That the agrarian revolution, and consequently also the general democratic revoluton, could be realized only by the united forces of the workers and peasants in struggle against the liberal bourgeoisie, was for me, contrary to all the senseless fairy tales of recent years, beyond any doubt. Yet I came out against the formula: "democratic dictatorship of the proletariat and peasantry", because I saw its shortcoming in the fact that it left open the question of what class the real dictatorship would belong to.

* Algebra deals with general quantities (a, b, c) in contrast to arithmetic which always employs definite quantities (1, 2, 3).

I endeavored to show that in spite of its enormous social and revolutionary weightiness, the peasantry was incapable of creating a really independent party and still more incapable of concentrating the revolutionary power in its hands. Just as the peasantry in the old revolutions since the German Reformation of the XVI century, and even before that, supported one of the fractions of the city bourgeois by its uprisings, and not infrequently insured its victory, so it could show a similar support in our belated bourgeois revolution at the highest swing of the struggle of the proletariat, and help it seize power. From this I drew the conclusion that our bourgeois revolution could solve its task radically only in the event that the proletariat, with the aid of the many-millioned peasantry, were capable of concentrating the revolutionary dictatorship in its hands.

What would be the social content of this dictatorship? First of all, it would have to carry out thoroughly the agrarian revoluton and the democratic transformation of the state. In other words, the dictatorship of the proletariat would be a means of solving the tasks of the historically belated bourgeois revolution. But the matter could not be confined to this. Having reached power, the proletariat would be compelled to encroach ever more deeply upon the relationships of private property in general, that is, to take the road of socialist measures.

"Do you perhaps believe", the Stalins, Rykovs and all the other Molotovs rejoined dozens of times from 1905 to 1917, "that Russia is ripe for the socialist revolution?" To that I always answered: No, I do not. But world economy as a whole, and European economy in the first place, is completely ripe for the socialist revolution. Whether the dictatorship of the proletariat in Russia leads to socialism or not, and at what rate and over what stages, will depend upon the further fate of European and international capitalism.

These were the essential features of the theory of the permanent revolution at its origin in the early months of 1905. Since then, three revolutions have taken place. The Russian proletariat ascended to power on the mighty wave of the peasant insurrection. The dictatorship of the proletariat became a fact in Russia earlier than in any other of the immeasurably more developed countries of the world. In 1924, that is, seven years after the historical prognosis of the theory of the permanent revolution was confirmed with rare force, the epigones opened up a wild attack against this theory, and plucked isolated sentences and polemical rejoinders out of my old works, which I had since completely forgotten.

It is appropriate to call to mind here that the first Russian revolution broke out more than half a century after the wave of bourgeois revolutions in Europe and thirty-five years after the episodic uprising of the Paris Commune. Europe had had time to disaccustom itself from revolutions. Russia had not experienced any. All the problems of the revolution had to be posed anew. It is not difficult to conceive how many unknown and putative quantities the future revolution held up for us in those days. The slogans of all the groupings were to a certain extent based upon hypotheses. A complete incapacity for historical prognoses and utter lack of understanding of their methods is required in order now, after the event, to consider analyses and evaluations of 1905 as though they were written yesterday. I have often said to myself and to my friends: I do not doubt that my prognoses of 1905 contained many defects which are not hard to disclose now, after the event. But did my critics see better and further? I had considered the defeats in my old works, which I had not perused for a long time, more serious and important than they really are. I convinced myself of that in 1928, when the political leisure imposed upon me in the banishment at Alma-Ata, afforded me the possibility to scrutinize with pencil in hand the old works on the permanent revolution. I hope that the reader too will be thoroughly convinced of this by what follows.

It is nevertheless necessary, within the limits of this introduction, to present as exact as possible a characterization of the elements of the theory of the permanent revolution and of the most important objections to it. The differences of opinion have become so broadened and deepened that they now actually embrace all the most important questions of the revolutionary world movement.

The permanent revolution, in the sense which Marx attached to the conception, means a revolution which makes no compromise with any form of class rule, which does not stop at the democratic stage, which goes over to socialist measures and to war against the reaction from without, that is, a revolution whose every next stage is anchored in the preceding one and which can only end in the complete liquidation of all class society.

To dispel the chaos that has been created around the theory of the permanent revolution, it is necessary to distinguish three lines of thought that are united in this theory.

First, it embraces the problem of the transition of the democratic revolution into the socialist. This is really the historical origin of the theory.

The conception of the permanent revolution was set up by the great Communists of the middle of the XIX century, by Marx and his adherents, in opposition to that democratic ideology which, as is known, presumed that all questions should be settled peacefully, in a reformist or evolutionary way, by the erection of the "rational" or democratic state. Marx regarded the bourgeois revolution of '48 as the direct introduction to the proletarian revolution. Marx "erred". Yet his error has a factual and not a methodological character. The revolution of 1848 did not turn into the socialist revolution. But that is just why it also did not achieve democracy. As to the German revolution of 1918, it is no democratic completion of the bourgeois revolution: it is a proletarian revolution decapitated by the social democracy; more correctly, it is the bourgeois *counter-revolution*, which is compelled to preserve pseudo-democratic forms after the victory over the proletariat.

Vulgar "Marxism" has worked out a schema of historical development, according to which every bourgeois society sooner or later secures a democratic régime, and after which it gradually organizes and raises the proletariat, under the conditions of democracy, to socialism. As to the transition to socialism itself, there have been various notions: the avowed reformists imagined this transition as the reformist cramming of democracy with a socialist content (Jaurès). The formal revolutionists acknowledged the inevitability of applying revolutionary violence in the transition to socialism (Guèsde). But both of them regarded democracy and socialism with regard to all peoples and countries as two not only entirely separated stages in the development of society, but also lying at great distances from each other. This view was predominant also among those Russian Marxists who, in the period of 1905, belonged to the Left wing of the Second International. Plechanov, the brilliant progenitor of Russian Marxism, considered the idea of the dictatorship of the proletariat a delusion in contemporary Russia. The same standpoint was defended not only by the Mensheviks, but also by the overwhelming majority of the leading Bolsheviks, among them all the present party leaders without exception, who at that time were resolute revolutionary democrats, for whom the problem of the socialist revolution, not only in 1905 but also on the eve of 1917, still signified the vague music of a distant future.

These ideas and moods declared war upon the theory of the permanent revolution, risen anew in 1905. It pointed out that the democratic tasks of the backward bourgeois nations in our epoch led to the dictatorship of the proletariat and that the dictatorship of the proletariat puts the socialist tasks on the order of the day. In that lay the central idea of the theory. If the traditional view was that the road to the dictatorship of the proletariat led through a long period of democracy, the theory of permanent revolution established the fact that for backward countries the road to democracy passed through the dictatorship of the proletariat. By that alone, democracy does not become a régime anchored within itself for decades, but rather a direct introduction to the socialist revolution. Each is bound to the other by an unbroken chain. In this way, there arises between the democratic revolution and the socialist transformation of society a permanency of revolutionary development.

The second aspect of the "permanent" theory already characterizes the socialist revolution as such. For an indefinitely long time and in constant internal struggle, all social relations are transformed. The process necessarily retains a political character, that is, it develops through collisions of various groups of society in transformation. Outbreaks of civil war and foreign wars alternate with periods of "peaceful" reforms. Revolutions in economy, technique, science, the family, morals and usages develop in complicated reciprocal action and do not allow society to reach equilibrium. Therein lies the permanent character of the socialist revolution as such.

The international character of the socialist revolution, which constitutes the third aspect of the theory of the permanent revolution, results from the present state of economy and the social structure of humanity. Internationalism is no abstract principle, but a theoretical and political reflection of the character of world economy, of the world development of productive forces, and the world scale of the class struggle. The socialist revolution begins on national grounds. But it cannot be completed on these grounds. The maintenance of the proletarian revolution within a national framework can only be a provisional state of affairs, even though, as the experience of the Soviet Union shows, one of long duration. In an isolated proletarian dictatorship, the internal and external contradictions grow inevitably together with the growing successes. Remaining isolated, the proletarian state must finally become a victim of these contradictions. The way out for it lies only in the victory of the proletariat of the advanced countries. Viewed from this standpoint, a national revolution is not a self-sufficient whole: it is only a link in the international chain. The international revolution presents a permanent process, in spite of all fleeting rises and falls.

The struggle of the epigones is directed, even if not always with the same distinctness, against all three aspects of the theory of the permanent revolution. And how could it be otherwise when it is a question of three inseparably connected parts of a whole. The epigones mechanically separate the *democratic* and the *socialist* dictatorships. They separate the *national* socialist revolution from the *international*. The conquest of power within national limits is considered by them in essence not as the initial act but as the final act of the revolution: after that follows the *period of reforms* which leads to the national socialist society. In 1905, they did not even grant the idea that the proletariat could conquer power in Russia earlier than in Western Europe. In 1917, they preached the self-sufficing democratic revolution in Russia and spurned the dictatorship of the proletariat. In 1925-1927, they steered a course towards the national revolution in China under the leadership of the bourgeoisie. Subsequently, they raised the slogan for China of the democratic dictatorship of the workers and peasants—in opposition to the dictatorship of the proletariat. They proclaimed the possibility of the construction of an isolated and self-sufficient socialist society in the Soviet Union. The world revolution became for them, instead of an indispensable pre-condition for victory, only a favorable circumstance. This profound breach with Marxism was reached by the epigones in the process of the permanent struggle against the theory of the permanent revolution.

The struggle, which began with an artificial revival of historical reminiscences and the falsification of the distant past, led to the complete transformation of the world outlook of the ruling stratum of the revolution. We have already repeatedly set forth that this transvaluation of values was accomplished under the influence of the social requirements of the Soviet bureaucracy, which became ever more conservative, strove for national order, and demanded that the already achieved revolution, which insured the privileged positions to the bureaucracy, now be considered adequate for the peaceful construction of socialism. We do not wish to return to this theme here. Let it simply be observed that the bureaucracy is deeply conscious of the connection of its material and ideological positions with the theory of national socialism. This is being expressed most crassly right now, in spite of or rather because of the fact that the Stalinist apparatus, under the pressure of contradictions which it did not foresee, is driving to the Left with all its might and inflicting quite severe blows upon its Right wing inspirers of yesterday. The hostility of the bureaucrats towards the Marxist Opposition, whose slogans and arguments they have borrowed in great haste, does not, as is known, diminish in the least. The condemnation of the theory of the permanent revolution above all, and an acknowledgment, even if only indirect, of the theory of socialism in one country, is demanded of the Oppositionists who raise the question of their re-admission into the party for the purpose of supporting the course towards industrialization, and so forth. By this, the Stalinist bureaucracy reveals the purely *tactical* character of its swing to the Left with the retention of the national reformist *strategical* foundations. It is superfluous to explain what this means; in politics as in the military affairs, tactics are subordinated in the long run, to strategy.

The question has long ago grown out of the specific sphere of the struggle against "Trotskyism". Gradually extending itself, it has today literally embraced all the problems of the revolutionary world outlook. Permanent revolution *or* socialism in one country—this alternative embraces at the same time the internal problems of the Soviet Union, the perspectives of the revolution in the East, and finally, the fate of the whole Communist International.

The present work does not examine this question from *all* sides: It is not necessary to repeat what has already been said in other works. In the *Criticism of the Program of the Communist International*, I have endeavored to disclose theoretically the economic and political untenability of national socialism. The theoreticians of the Comintern were as silent about it as though their mouths were filled with water. That is perhaps the only thing left for them to do. In this booklet, I above all restore the theory of the permanent revolution as it was formulated in 1905 with regard to the internal problems of the Russian revolution. I show wherein my position actually differed from Lenin's, and how and why it coincided with Lenin's position in every decisive situation. Finally, I endeavor to reveal the decisive significance of the question that interests us here for the proletariat of the backward countries, and thereby, for the Communist International as a whole.

* * *

What accusations have been raised against the theory of the permanent revolution by the epigones? Disregard the innumerable contradictions of my critics, and their whole, veritably immense, literature can be reproduced in the following sentences:

1. Trotsky ignored the difference between the bourgeois revolution and the socialist; already in 1905 he

represented the standpoint that the proletariat of Russia stands before the tasks of a directly socialist revolution.

2. Trotsky completely forgot the agrarian question. The peasantry did not exist for him. He depicted the revolution as a duel between the proletariat and czarism.

3. Trotsky did not believe that the world bourgeoisie would stand for a somewhat lengthy existence of the dictatorship of the Russian proletariat and regarded its fall as inevitable in the event that the proletariat of the West did not seize power within the briefest period and provide assistance. By this Trotsky under-evaluated the pressure of the Western European proletariat upon its own bourgeoisie.

4. Trotsky does not believe altogether in the power of the Russian proletariat, nor in its ability to construct socialism independently, and that is why he has put and still puts all his hopes in the international revolution.

These motifs run through not only the numberless writings and speeches of Zinoviev, Stalin, Bucharin and others, but they are also formulated in the most authoritative resolutions of the Communist Party of the Soviet Union and the Communist International. And in spite of that, one is compelled to say that they are based upon a mixture of ignorance and dishonesty.

The first two contentions of the critics are, as will be shown later on, false to the roots. No, I proceeded precisely from the bourgeois-democratic character of the revolution and arrived at the conclusion that the profundity of the agrarian crisis can raise to power the proletariat of backward Russia. Yes, these are just the ideas that I defended on the eve of the 1905 revolution. These are just the ideas that alone expressed the characterizaton of the revolution as a "permanent" one, that is, an uninterrupted one, that is, a revolution that passes over directly from the bourgeois stage into the socialist. To express the same ideas, Lenin later used the excellent expression of the bourgeois revolution—"*growing into*" the socialist. The conception of the growing into was contrasted by Stalin, after the event (in 1924), to the permanent revolution as a direct leap from the realm of autocracy into the realm of socialism. The unfortunate "theoretician" did not even take the trouble to reflect, if it is simply a matter of a *leap*, what the *permanency* of the revolution means!

As for the third accusation, it was dictated by the short-lived belief of the epigones in the possibility of *neutralizing* the imperialist bourgeoisie for an unlimited time with the aid of the "shrewdly" organized pressure of the proletariat. In the years 1924-1927 this was the central idea of Stalin. The Anglo-Russian Committee then became its fruit. The disappointment of the possibility of binding the world bourgeoisie hand and foot with the help of Purcell, Raditch, La Follette and Chiang Kai-Shek, led to an acute paroxysm of fear of an immediate war danger. The Comintern is still passing through this period.

The fourth objection to the theory of the permanent revolution simply amounts to saying that I did not defend the standpoint of the theory of socialism in one country in 1905, which Stalin first manufactured in 1924 for the Soviet bureaucracy. This accusation should be appreciated only as a historical curiosity. One might actually believe that my critics in so far as they thought of anything at all in 1905, were of the opinion then that Russia was prepared for an independent socialist revolution. As a matter of fact, however, they accused me tirelessly in the period of 1905 to 1917 of Utopianism, because I counted upon the probability that the Russian proletariat could come to power before the proletariat of Western Europe. Kamenev and Rykov accused Lenin of Utopianism in April 1917, using against him the vulgar argument that the socialist revolution must first be achieved in England and in the other advanced countries before it could be Russia's turn. The same standpoint was defended by Stalin too, up to April 4, 1917. Only gradually and with difficulty, did he adopt the Leninist formula of the dictatorship of the proletariat in contradistinction to the democratic dictatorship. In the spring of 1924, Stalin was still repeating what the others had said before him: isolated, Russia is not mature for the construction of a socialist society. In the autumn of 1924, Stalin, in his *struggle* against the theory of the permanent revolution, for the first time discovered the possibility of building up an isolated socialism in Russia. Only then did the Red professors collect quotations for Stalin which convict Trotsky of having believed in 1905— how terrible!—that Russia could reach socialism only with the aid of the proletariat of Western Europe.

Were one to take the history of an ideological struggle over a period of a quarter of a century, cut it into little pieces, mix them up in a mortar, and then command a blind man to paste the pieces together again, a greater theoretical and historical absurdity could hardly result than the one with which the epigones feed their readers and hearers.

* * *

For the connection of yesterday's problems with today's to stand out more clearly one must recall here, even if only quite generally, what the leadership of the Comintern, that is, Stalin and Bucharin, carried out in China.

Under the pretext that China stands before a national revolution, the leading rôle was allotted to the Chinese bourgeoisie in 1924. The party of the national bourgeoisie, the Kuo Min Tang, was officially recognized as the leading party. Not even the Russian Mensheviks went that far in 1905 in relation to the Cadets (the party of the liberal bourgeoisie).

But the leadership of the Comintern did not stop at this. It obligated the Chinese Communist Party to go into the Kuo Min Tang and subordinate itself to its discipline. Through special telegrams of Stalin, the Chinese Communists were urged to curb the agrarian movement. The mutinous workers and peasants were prohibited from forming their own Soviets in order not to alienate Chiang Kai-Shek, whom Stalin defended against the Oppositionists as a "reliable ally" at a party meeting in Moscow at the beginning of April 1927, that is, a few days before the counter-revolutionary *coup d'État* in Shanghai.

The official subjugation of the Communist party to the bourgeois leadership and the official prohibition to form Soviets (Stalin and Bucharin taught that the Kuo Min Tang "substituted" for Soviets), was a grosser and more crying betrayal of Marxism than all the deeds of the Mensheviks in the years 1905-1917.

After Chiang Kai-Shek's *coup d'État* in April 1927, a Left wing, under the leadership of Wang Chin Wei split off temporarily from the Kuo Min Tang. Wang Chin Wei was immedately hailed in PRAVDA as a reliable ally. In essence, Wang Chin Wei bore the same relation to Chiang Kai-Shek as Kerensky to Miliukov, with the difference that, in China, Miliukov and Kornilov were united in the person of Chiang Kai-Shek.

After April 1927, the Chinese party was ordered to go into the "Left" Kuo Min Tang and to subordinate itself to the discipline of the Chinese Kerensky instead of preparing open warfare against him. The "reliable" Wang Chin Wei crushed the Communist party together with the workers' and peasants' movement no less criminally than Chiang Kai-Shek, whom Stalin had declared as his reliable ally.

When the Mensheviks supported Miliukov in 1905 and afterwards, they nevertheless did not enter the liberal party. When the Mensheviks went hand in hand with Kerensky in 1917, they still retained their own organization. The policy of Stalin in China was a wretched caricature even of Menshevism. That is what the first and most important period looked like.

After its inevitable fruits had appeared: complete decline of the workers' and peasants' movement, demoralization and decay of the Communist party, the leadership of the Comintern gave the command: "Left about face!" and demanded the immediate armed uprising of the workers and peasants. In this way, the young, oppressed and mutilated Communist party, which only yesterday was the fifth wheel in the wagon of Chiang Kai-Shek and Wang Chin Wei, and consequently did not possess the slightest political experience of its own, was handed the order to lead the workers and peasants—whom the Comintern had held back up to yesterday in the name of the Kuo Min Tang—in an armed insurrection against the same Kuo Min Tang, which had in the meanwhile found time to concentrate the power and the army in its hands. In the course of twenty-four hours a fictitious Soviet was improvised in Canton. The armed insurrection, timed in advance for the opening of the Fifteenth Congress

of the Communist party of the Soviet Union, constituted simultaneously an expression of the heroism of
the vanguard of the Chinese proletariat as well as of
the crime of the Comintern. Lesser adventures pre-
ceded the Canton uprising and followed it. That is
what the second chapter of the Chinese strategy of the
Comintern looked like, a strategy that can be characterized as the most malicious caricature of Bolshevism.

The liberal-opportunist, as well as the adventurist
chapter, delivered a blow to the Chinese Communist
Party from which, even with a correct policy, it can
recover only after a long period.

The Sixth Congress of the Comintern drew the
balance to this work. It approved it entirely, which
is not very astonishing: it was for this purpose that it
was convoked. For the future, the Congress set up
the slogan "democratic dictatorship of the proletariat and peasantry". By what this dictatorship is to
be distinguished from the dictatorship of the Right
and Left Kuo Min Tang on the one side, and the dictatorship of the proletariat on the other, was not explained to the Chinese Communists. Nor is it possible to explain it.

Issuing the slogan of the democratic dictatorship,
the Sixth Congress at the same time declared the slogans of democracy inadmissible (constituent assembly, universal suffrage, freedom of press and assembly, etc., etc.), and it thereby completely disarmed the
Chinese Communist Party in the face of the dictatorship of the military oligarchy. For a long number of
years, the Russian Bolsheviks mobilized the workers
and peasants around the slogans of democracy. The
slogans of democracy also played a big rôle in 1917.
Only after the already really existing Soviet power
had arrived at an irreconcilable political antagonism

to the Constituent Assembly before the eyes of the entire people, did our party liquidate the institutions and slogans of formal, that is, of bourgeois democracy, in favor of real Soviet, that is, of proletarian democracy.

The Sixth Congress of the Comintern, under the direction of Stalin and Bucharin, turned all this on its head. While, on the one hand, it prescribed "democratic" and not "proletarian" dictatorship for the party, it simultaneously forbade it the democratic slogans for preparing this dictatorship. The Chinese Communist Party was not only disarmed, but stripped naked. But for that, it was finally handed as consolation, in the period of unlimited domination of the counter-revolution, the slogan of Soviets, which had been prohibited at the time of the revolutionary ascent. A very popular hero of a Russian folk tale sings wedding songs at funerals and funeral hymns at weddings. He gets a sound thrashing in both places. If the thing were limited to a sound thrashing for the present leaders of the Comintern, one might let it go at that. But the stakes are far greater. It is the fate of the proletariat that is involved. The tactics of the Comintern was an unconsciously, but all the more surely, organized sabotage of the Chinese revolution. This sabotage was accomplished without any hindrance, for the Right Menshevik policy of the Comintern in the years 1924-1927 was clothed in all the authority of Bolshevism and protected by the Soviet power through the immense machinery of reprisals against the criticism of the Left Opposition.

As a result, we received a perfect example of Stalinist strategy, which stood from beginning to end under the insignia of the struggle against the permanent revolution. It is therefore quite in place for the principal Stalinist theoretician of the subordination of the Chinese Communist Party to the national bourgeois Kuo Min Tang to have been Martinov, that is, the principal Menshevik critic of the theory of the permanent revolution from 1905 to 1923, when he already began to fulfill his historic mission in the ranks of Bolshevism.

* * *

The essentials on the origin of the present work have been dealt with in the first chapter. In Alma-Ata, I was very calmly preparing a theoretical polemic against the epigones. The theory of the permanent revolution was to occupy a large place in the book. While at work, I received a manuscript of Radek's, which occupied itself with contrasting the permanent revolution with the strategic line of Lenin. Radek needed this apparently sudden sortie because he was himself submerged up to his ears in Stalin's Chinese politics: Radek (together with Zinoviev) preached the subordination of the Communist party to the Kuo Min Tang not only before Chiang Kai-Shek's *coup d'État* but even after it.

In support of the enslavement of the proletariat to the bourgeoisie, Radek naturally referred to the necessity of an alliance with the peasantry and to the "underestimation" of this necessity by me. After Stalin, he too defended the Menshevik policy with Bolshevik phraseology. With the formula of the democratic dictatorship of the proletariat and the peasantry, Radek, following Stalin in this, cloaked the diversion of the Chinese proletariat from leading the independent struggle for power at the head of the peasant masses. When I exposed this ideological masquerade, there arose in Radek the urgent need to prove, painted up with quotations from Lenin, that my struggle against opportunism resulted in reality from the antagonism between the theory of the permanent revolution and Leninism. Radek converted the lawyer-like defense of his own offense into a prosecutor's speech against the permanent revolution. This appearance was only a bridge to capitulation for him. I might have surmised this with all the more justice since Radek, years before, had planned to write a brochure in defense of the permanent revolution. Still I did not hasten to make a cross over Radek. I undertook the attempt to answer his article in all frankness and resolution, without cutting off his retreat. I print my reply to Radek just as it was written, and confine myself to a few explanatory supplements and stylistic corrections.

Radek's article was not published in the press, and I believe it will not be published, for in the form in which it was written in 1928 it could not pass the sieve of the Stalinist censor. But even for Radek himself this article would be downright annihilating today, for it would give a glaring picture of Radek's ideological evolution which very strongly recalls the "evolution" of a man who throws himself out of the sixth story.

The origin of this work explains sufficiently why Radek probably occupies a larger place in it than it is his right to claim. Radek himself did not think up a single argument against the theory of the permanent revolution. He only came forward as an epigone of the epigones. The reader is therefore recommended to see in Radek not simply Radek but the representative of a certain corporation, a not fully qualified membership in which he purchased at the price of a renunciation of Marxism. Should Radek personally feel, in spite of this, that too many digs have fallen to his share, then he should turn them over to

the right address at his own discretion. That is a
private affair of the firm. On my part, I raise no
objections.

PRINKIPO, *November 30, 1930* L. Trotsky

I

The Enforced Character of This Work and

Its Aim

*T*HE THEORETICAL needs of the party led by the Right-Centrist bloc were covered for six successive years by anti-Trotskyism: the only product present in an unlimited amount and available for free distribution. Stalin associated himself with a "theory" for the first time in 1924, with his immortal articles against the permanent revolution. Even Molotov was baptized as a "leader" in this basin. The falsification is in full swing. A few days ago I happened across an announcement of the publication of Lenin's works of 1917 in the German language. This is an invaluable gift to the advanced German working class. One can, however, just picture from the very outset how many falsifications there will be in the text, and especially in the annotations. It is enough to point out that the first place in the table of contents in assigned to *Lenin's* letters to Kollontai (in New York). Why? Because these letters contain harsh remarks about me, based on completely *false information* of Kollontai, who gave her organic Menshevism a hysterical ultra-Left inoculation in those days. In the Russian edition, the epigones were compelled to indicate, at least ambiguously, that Lenin had been falsely informed. It may be assumed without further ado that the German edition will not present even this evasive reservation. It must still be added that in the same letters of Lenin to Kollontai there are furious assaults upon Bucharin, with whom Kollontai was then in solidarity. This part of the letter, at any rate, has been suppressed for the time being. We will not have to wait very long for it*. On the other hand, valuable documents, articles and speeches of Lenin, as well as minutes, letters, and so forth, remain concealed only because they are directed against Stalin and Co., and undermine the legend of Trotskyism. Of the history of the three Russian revolutions, as well as the history of the party, literally not a single shred has been left intact: theory, facts, traditions, the heritage of Lenin, all this has been sacrificed to the "struggle against Trotskyism", which, since Lenin was taken ill, was invented and organized as a personal struggle against Trotsky, and developed into struggle against Marxism.

It has again been confirmed that what might appear as the most useless raking up of long extinct disputes usually satisfies some unconscious social requirement of the day, a requirement which, by itself, does not follow the line of the old disputes. The campaign against "old Trotskyism" was in reality the campaign against the October traditions, which are felt as obstructive and unbearable by the new bureaucracy. They began to characterize as "Trotskyism" everything they wanted to be rid of. Thus the strug-

* This prophecy has in the meantime been fulfilled.

gle against Trotskyism gradually became the expression of the theoretical and political *reaction* in the broadest non-proletarian, and partly also in the proletarian, circles, as well as the expression of this reaction inside the party. An especially caricatured, historically falsified contrast of the permanent revolution with Lenin's line with regard to the "alliance with the peasants" arose in 1923, together with the period of the general reaction as well as the internal party reaction, as the consummate expression and the most organized renunciation by the bureaucrat and the petty bourgeois of the international revolution with its "'permanent" convulsions, as the expression of the petty bourgeois and bureaucratic propensity for peace and order. The vicious baiting of the permanent revolution, in turn, came up only as the preparation of the ground for the theory of the revolution in one country, that is, for national-socialism of the latest type. It is understood that by themselves these new social roots of the struggle against "Trotskyism" do not prove anything either for or against the correctness of the permanent revolution. Yet, without an understanding of these hidden roots the struggle must always bear a barren academic character.

I was not in a position to compel myself in recent years to put aside the new problems and turn my attention to the old questions that are bound up with the period of the revolution of 1905, mainly in so far as they concern my past and are artifically directed against it. An analysis of the old differences of opinion, among others, my old mistakes in connection with the situation out of which they arose, an analysis so thorough that it becomes comprehensible to the young generation, not to speak of the old one that has fallen into political childhood, is only possible within the

limits of a more voluminous book. It seemed monstrous to me to waste my own and others' time upon it,
where constantly new tasks of gigantic stature were
arising: the tasks of the German revolution, the question of the future fate of England, the question of the
mutual relations between America and Europe, the
problems made acute by the strikes of the British proletariat, the tasks of the Chinese revolution and, lastly
and mainly, our own internal economic and socio-
political antagonisms and tasks—all this, I believe,
amply justifies putting aside my historico-polemical
work on the permanent revolution.   But the social
consciousness tolerates no omissions.   In recent years,
as has been said, this theoretical omission was
filled up with the rubbish of anti-Trotskyism.   The
epigones, the philosophers and the henchmen of party
reaction slipped down ever lower, went to school to
the dull-witted Menshevik, Martinov, trampled Lenin
under foot, floundered around in the swamp, and called
it all the struggle against Trotskyism.   All these
years they have been incapable of producing even a
single work, serious and important enough to be pronounced without shame a political examination of lasting significance, a prognosis that has been confirmed,
an independent slogan that has advanced us ideologically.   Everywhere only decay and nonsense.

Stalin's *Problems of Leninism* constitute a modifica-
tion of mental refuse, an official manual of narrow-
mindedness, a collection of enumerated banalities (I am
doing my best to find the most moderate designations).
Leninism by Zinoviev is . . . Zinovievist Leninism,
no more and no less.   The occupation with all these
theoretical fruits of epigonism is equally unbearable,
with one distinction: a reading of Zinoviev's *Leninism*
is like choking on fluffy cotton, while Stalin's *Problems*

arouses the physical feeling of a throat filled with chopped up bristles. These two books are, each in its own way, the image and crown of the epoch of ideological reaction.

Applying every question—whether from the Right or the Left, from above or below, from before or behind—to Trotskyism, the epigones have finally understood how to make every world event directly or indirectly dependent upon how the permanent revolution looked to Trotsky in 1905. The legend of Trotskyism, chock full of falsifications, became to a certain extent a factor in contemporary history. And while the Right-Centrist line of recent years has compromised itself in every continent by bankruptcies of historical dimensions, the struggle against the Centrist ideology in the Comintern is today already unthinkable, or at least made very difficult, without a correct evaluation of the old disputed questions and prognoses that originated in the beginning of 1905.

The resurrection of Marxian, and consequently Leninist, thought in the party is unthinkable without a polemical annihilation of the scribblings of the epigones, without a merciless theoretical execution of the apparatus-executioners. It is really not difficult to write such a book. All its ingredients are at hand. Nevertheless, it is hard to write such a book, because in doing it one must, in the words of the great satirist, Saltykov. descend into the domain of "A B C effluvia" and dwell for a while in this scarcely ambrosial atmosphere. But the work is absolutely unpostponable, for it is precisely upon the struggle against the permanent revolution that the defense of the opportunist line in the problems of the East, that is, the larger half of humanity, is directly constructed.

I was already on the point of entering into the

hardly alluring work of a theoretical polemic with
Zinoviev and Stalin, and of laying by the books of our
classicists for recreation hours (even divers must rise
to the surface now and then to breathe a draught of
fresh air) when, quite unexpectedly for me, an article
by Radek appeared and began to circulate, devoted
to the "more profound" contrast of the theory of the
permanent revolution with the views of Lenin on this
subject. At the beginning, I wanted to ignore Radek's
work, so as not to avoid the portion of fluffy cotton
and chopped up bristles intended for me by destiny.
But a number of letters from friends induced me to
read Radek's work more attentively, and I came to
the following conclusion: for a more intimate circle
of persons who are capable of thinking independently,
and not upon command, and have conscientiously studied Marxism, Radek's work is more dangerous than the
official literature—just as opportunism in politics is
all the more dangerous the more veiled it appears and
the greater the personal prominence that covers it.
Radek is one of my closest political friends. This has
been amply witnessed by the events of the latest period.
In recent months, however, various comrades have followed with misgivings the evolution of Radek, which
has shifted him from the extreme Left wing of the
Opposition to the tip of its Right wing. We, the intimate friends of Radek, know that his brilliant political and literary capacities, which are united with a
rare impulsiveness and sensitiveness, are qualities
which constitute a valuable source of initiative and
criticism under the conditions of isolation. Radek's
latest work—in connection with his actions preceding
it—leads to the judgment that Radek has lost the
compass, or rather that his compass is under the
influence of a steady magnetic disturbance. Radek's

work is in no sense an episodic excursion into the past;
no, it is an insufficiently thought out, but because of
that, a no less harmful support of the official course,
with all its theoretical mythology.

The above-characterized political function of the
present struggle against "Trotskyism" naturally does
not in any way signify that within the Opposition,
which has developed as the Marxian point of support
against the ideological and political reaction, a criticism is inadmissible, especially a criticism of my old
differences of opinion with Lenin. On the contrary,
such a work of clarification could only be fruitful. But
herewith, a scrupulous preservation of the historical
perspective, a serious investigation of the source and
an illumination of the past differences in the light of
the present struggle would be absolutely necessary.
There is not a trace of all this in Radek. Assuming
an unsuspecting air, he joins in the chain fighting
against "Trotskyism", utilizing not only the one-
sidedly selected quotations, but also their radically
false official interpretations. Where he seemingly
separates himself from the official campaign, he does
it in so ambiguous a manner that he really provides
it with the two-fold aid of an "impartial" witness. As
always happens in a case of spiritual decay, the latest
work of Radek does not contain a single trace of his
political penetration and his literary skill. It is a
work without perspectives, without the three dimensions, a work on the level of the quotations, and therefore—a *superficial* work.

Out of what political requirements was it born? Out
of the differences of opinion that arose between Radek
and the overwhelming majority of the Opposition in
the questions of the Chinese revolution. A few voices
are heard, it is true, that the differences of opinion on

China are "not timely" (Preobrazhensky). But these
voices do not even deserve serious consideration.   The
whole of Bolshevism grew and eventually gathered
strength on the criticism and the assimilation of the
experiences of 1905, in all their freshness, while these
experiences were still an *immediate experience* of the
first generation of Bolsheviks.   How could it be otherwise, for out of what other event could the new gen-
erations of the proletarian revolutionists learn if not
from the fresh, warm experiences of the Chinese revolution, still reeking with blood?   Only lifeless ped-
ants are capable of "postponing" the questions of the
Chinese revolution, in order to "study" them later on
in all peace, in their leisure hours.   It becomes Bol-
shevik-Leninists all the less since the revolutions in the
countries of the East have in no sense been removed
from the order of the day and the periods between
are not yet known to anybody.

Adopting a false position in the problems of the
Chinese revolution, Radek endeavors, after the event,
to establish this position by a one-sided and distorted
presentation of my old differences of opinion with
Lenin.   And this is where Radek is compelled to
borrow his weapons from strange arsenals and to swim
without a compass in strange waters.

Radek is my friend, but the truth is dearer to me.
I feel myself obliged to set aside the more extensive
work on the problems of the revolution in order to refute Radek.   It involves too important questions,
raised with extreme sharpness.   I have a threefold
difficulty to overcome here: the number and multiplicity of the errors in Radek's work; the profusion of
literary and historical facts out of the twenty-three
years (1905-1928) that refute Radek; and thirdly,
the brevity of the time that I can devote to this work,

for the economic problems of the U. S. S. R. are
pressing to the foreground.

These circumstances determine the character and
scope of the present work.   It does not exhaust the
question.   There is much in it that remains unexpres-
sed—in part, at any rate, also because it is connected
with preceding works, primarily *The Criticism of the
Program of the Communist International*.   Mountains
of factual material which I have assembled on this
question remain unused—up to the writing of the contemplated book against the epigones, that is, against
the ideology of the period of reaction.

* * *

Radek's work on the permanent revolution culmin-
ates with the conclusion:

"*The new section of the party (Opposition) is
threatened with the danger of the rise of tendencies
which, in the course of time, will tear the proletarian
revolution away from its allies— the peasantry.*"

It is dumbfounding at first sight that this conclusion should be issued in the second half of 1928 as a
new conclusion with regard to the "new" section of
the party.   We have been aware of it without inter-
ruption since the spring of 1923. But how does Radek
motivate his turn to the official principal thesis? Again,
not in a new way: he turns back to the theory of the
permanent revolution.   In 1924-1925, Radek more
than once intended to write a pamphlet which was to
be dedicated to the idea of demonstrating that the
theory of the permanent revolution and the Leninist
slogan of the democratic dictatorship of the proletariat and peasantry, regarded on an historical scale, that
is, in the light of the three revolutions passed through
by us, could in no case be contrasted to each other,

but were. on the contrary, identical in essence. Now,
after having thoroughly examined the question—as he
writes one of his friends—"anew", Radek has reached
the conclusion that the old theory of permanency
threatens the "new" section of the party with nothing
more nor less than the danger of separation from the
peasantry.

But how did Radek thoroughly examine this question? He gives us some information on this point:

"We do not have at hand the formulations which
Trotsky presented in 1905 in a preface to Marx's
Civil War in France and in 1905 in *Our Revolution.*"

The years are not correctly quoted here, it is true,
yet it is not worth while to dwell upon it. It is a
matter of fact that the only work in which I presented
my views more or less systematically on the development of the revolution at that time, is a rather extensive essay: *Results and Perspectives* (*Our Revolution*, Petersburg, 1906, pages 224-286). The article in the Polish organ of Rosa Luxemburg and
Tyschko (1909), to which Radek refers, but unfortunately interprets in Kamenev's sense, lays no claim
to completeness and comprehensiveness. Theoretically,
this work is based upon the above-mentioned book *Our
Revolution*. Nobody is obligated to read this book
now. Since that time, such great events have taken
place and we have learned so much from these events
that, truth to tell, I feel an aversion to the manner
of the epigones of considering new historical problems
not in the light of living experiences of the revolutions
already carried out by us, but mainly in the light of
quotations that refer to our prognoses on *future* revolutions. Naturally, by this I do not want to deprive
Radek of the right to take up the question from the
historico-literary side also. But in that case, it must

be done in the right way. Radek undertakes the attempt to illuminate the fate of the theory of the permanent revolution in the course of a quarter of a century, and remarks by the by that he "has not at hand" precisely those words in which I set down this theory.

I want to point out right here that Lenin, as has become particularly clear to me now by reading his old works, did not read the above-mentioned fundamental article. This is probably not to be explained only by the fact that *Our Revolution*, which appeared in 1906, was immediately confiscated, and that we went into emigration, but also by the fact that two-thirds of the book consisted of reprints of old articles. I heard later from many comrades that they had not read this book because they thought it consisted exclusively of reprints of old works. In any case, the few scattered polemical remarks of Lenin against the permanent revolution rest exclusively upon the foreword of Parvus to my pamphlet, *Until the Ninth of January*, further, upon Parvus' proclamation *No Czars!*, which remained completely unknown to me, and upon inner-party differences of Lenin with Bucharin and others. Never did Lenin anywhere analyze, be it even in passing, *Results and Perspectives*, and a few replies of Lenin to the permanent revolution, obviously referring to me, directly prove that he did not read this work*.

It would be wrong to believe, however, that this is

---

* In 1909, Lenin did indeed quote my "Results and Perspectives", in an article intended as a polemic against Martov. It would not, however, be difficult to prove that Lenin took over the quotations at second hand, that is, from Martov in this case. This is the only way that certain of his replies directed at me, which are based upon obvious misunderstandings, can be explained.

In 1919, the State Publishing House issued my "Results and

just what Lenin's "Leninism" consists of. But this
seems to be the opinion of Radek. In any case, Radek's
article which I have to examine here shows not only
that he did "not have at hand" my fundamental works,
but also that he never even read them. If he did, then
it was long ago, before the October revolution. In
any case he did not retain much of it in his memory.

But the matter does not end there. Even though
it was admissible and even unavoidable in 1905 or 1909
to polemicize over a few articles that were timely then
and even over single sentences in single articles taken

Perspectives" as a special pamphlet. The annotation to the
complete edition of Lenin's works, which is to the effect
that the theory of the permanent revolution is especially noteworthy "now", after the October revolution, dates back to
approximately the same time. Did Lenin read my "Results
and Perspectives" in 1919, or merely glance through it? On
this I cannot say anything definite. I was then constantly
traveling, came to Moscow only for short stays, and during
my meetings with Lenin in that period—at the height of the
civil war—factional theoretical reminiscences never entered
our minds. But A. A. Joffe did have a conversation with
Lenin, just at that time, on the theory of the permanent
revolution. Joffe reported this conversation in the farewell
letter he wrote me before his death. (See "My Life", Scrib-
ners, New York, page 537.) Can A. A. Joffe's assertions be
construed that Lenin in 1919 became acquainted f o r t h e
f i r s t t i m e with "Results and Perspectives" and confirmed
the correctness of the historical prognosis contained in it?
On this matter I can only express psychological conjectures.
The power of conviction of these conjectures depends upon
the evaluation of the kernel of the disputed question itself.
A. A. Joffe's words, that Lenin had confirmed my prognosis
as correct. must appear incomprehensible to a man who has
been raised upon the theoretical margarine of the post-Lenin-
ist epoch. On the other hand, whoever reflects upon the
evolution of Lenin's ideas in connection with the development
of the revolution itself, will understand that Lenin, in 1919,

together, especially under the conditions of the split, then a revolutionary Marxist today, should he want to look back over an enormous historical period, must put the question: How were the formulæ in question applied in practise, how were they construed in application? How were the *tactics?* Had Radek taken the trouble to glance through only the two volumes of *Our First Revolution* (*Collected Works*) he would not have found the courage to write his present work, at all events, he would have struck out a whole series of his impetuous contentions. At least, I hope he would.

had to deliver a new judgment on the theory of the permanent revolution, different from the ones he pronounced fleetingly, in passing, often manifestly self-contradictory, at various times before the October revolution, on the basis of isolated quotations without even once examining my position as a whole.

In order to confirm my prognosis as correct in 1919, Lenin did not need to contrast my position to his. It sufficed to consider both positions in their historical development. It is not necessary to repeat here that the concrete content with which Lenin always invested his formula of "democratic dictatorship" and which resulted less from a hypothetical formula than from the analysis of the actual changes in class relationships of forces—that this tactical and organizational content has passed once and for all into the inventory of history as a classic example of revolutionary realism. In almost all the cases, at any rate in all the important cases, where I placed myself in contradiction to Lenin tactically or organizationally, the right was on his side. That is just why it did not interest me to come forward for my old historical prognosis, so long as it might appear that it was only a matter of historical reminiscences. I found myself compelled to return to this question only at the moment when the criticism of the epigones of the theory of the permanent revolution not only began to nurture the theoretical reaction of the whole International, but also became converted into a means of the direct sabotage of the Chinese revolution.

From these two books, Radek would have learned, in the first place, that in my political activity the permanent revolution in no case signified for me a jumping over the democratic stage of the revolution or its specific steps. He could have convinced himself that, though I lived in Russia illegally throughout 1905 without connections with the emigration, I formulated the successive stages of the revolution in the same manner as Lenin: he could have learned that the fundamental appeals to the peasants that were issued by the central press of the Bolsheviks in 1905 were written by me; that the Novaïa Zhizn [New Life] edited by Lenin in an editorial note resolutely defended my articles on the permanent revolution which appeared in Natchalo [The Beginning]; that Lenin's Novaïa Zhizn and now and then Lenin himself supported and defended the political decisions of the Soviets of Deputies whose author I was and which I represented as reporter nine times out of ten; that, after the December defeat, I wrote a pamphlet on tactics in prison in which I pointed out the connection of the proletarian offensive with the agrarian revolution of the peasants as the central strategical problem; that Lenin published this pamphlet in the Bolshevik publishing house *Novaïa Volna* [New Wave] and had me informed of his hearty accord through Knunianz; that Lenin spoke at the London congress in 1907 of my "solidarity" with Bolshevism in the viewpoint on the peasantry and the liberal bourgeoisie. None of the exists for Radek: probably he did not have this "at hand" either.

How does the matter stand with Radek in relation to the works of Lenin? No better, or not much better. Radek confines himself to those quotations which Lenin did indeed direct against me but meant for others (for example, Bucharin and Radek: an open reference to this is found in Radek himself). Radek was unable to adduce a single new quotation: he simply made use of the finished quotation material that almost every citizen of the U. S. S. R. has "at hand". Radek only added a few quotations in which Lenin elucidated the elementary truths to the anarchists and Social Revolutionists on the difference between a bourgeois republic and socialism, where it looks as though these lines were directed against me. Hardly credible, but it is true.

Radek entirely avoids those old declarations in which Lenin, very cautiously and very sparingly, but with all the greater emphasis, established my solidarity with Bolshevism in questions of revolutionary principle. Here it must not be forgotten for an instant that Lenin did this at a time when I did not belong to the Bolshevik faction and that Lenin attacked me mercilessly (and rightly so) for my conciliationism —not for the permanent revolution, where he confined himself to occasional rejoinders—but for my conciliationism, for my readiness to hope for an evolution of the Mensheviks to the Left. Lenin was much more concerned with the struggle against conciliationism than with "justifying" single polemical blows against the "conciliator" Trotsky.

In 1924, defending before me Zinoviev's conduct in October 1917, Stalin wrote:

"Comrade Trotsky has not understood the letters of Lenin [on Zinoviev—L. T.], their significance and their destination. Lenin frequently used to rush ahead deliberately in his letters and to shove to the foreground the possible errors that might be made. He criticized them in advance with the aim of warning the party and insuring it against mistakes, or he often

exaggerated a 'trifle' and, with the same pedagogical
aim, made 'an elephant out of a gnat' . . . But to
draw from these letters of Lenin (and there are no
few such letters of his) the conclusion of 'tragic' differences of opinion and to trumpet this abroad—means
not to understand Lenin's letters, not to know Lenin."
(J. Stalin, *Trotskyism or Leninism*, 1924.)

However clumsy the formulation—"the style is the
man"—the ideas are nevertheless essentially correct,
even if they apply least of all precisely to the differences of opinion on October 1917, which do not quite
resemble a "gnat". But if Lenin used to resort to
"pedagogical" exaggerations and to preventive policies towards the closest members of his own faction,
then surely all the more so towards one who stood
outside the Bolshevik faction at the same time and
preached conciliationism. It never occurred to Radek
to allow for this corrective coefficient in the old quotations.

In 1922, I wrote in the foreword to my book *1905*
that my prognosis that the dictatorship of the proletariat is likely and possible in Russia sooner than in
the advanced countries, had been confirmed after
twelve years, Radek, following a not very seductive example, describes it as though I had *contrasted* this
prognosis with Lenin's strategical line. From the
foreword, however, it can be clearly seen that I considered the prognosis in those of its basic features in
which it *coincided* with the strategic line of Bolshevism. When I speak in a footnote of the "re-armament" of the party at the beginning of 1917, then it
is certainly not in the sense that Lenin recognized the
previous road of the party as "erroneous" but rather
that Lenin, even though after a delay, yet opportunely
enough for the success of the revolution, came to Rus-

sia to teach the party to *liberate* itself from the *outlived slogan* of the "democratic dictatorship" to which the Stalins, Kamenevs, Rykovs, Molotovs and others were still clinging. When the Kamenevs grow indignant at the mention of the "re-armament", it is comprehensible, for it was undertaken against them. But Radek? He first began to grow indignant in 1928, that is, only after he himself had begun to fight against the necessary "re-armament" of the Chinese Communist Party.

We would like to remind Radek that my books *1905* (with the indicated foreword) and *The October Revolution* played the rôle, while Lenin was alive, of the fundamental historical textbooks of the two revolutions. At that time, they went through innumerable editions in the Russian as well as in foreign languages. Never did anybody tell me that my books contain a contrast of two lines, because at that time, before the revisionist change of course by the epigones, every normal-thinking party member did not consider the October experiences in the light of the old quotations, but the old quotations in the light of the October revolution.

In connection with this there is still another point which Radek misuses in an impermissible manner: Trotsky did acknowledge—he says—that Lenin was right against him. True, he did acknowledge that. And in this acknowledgment there was not one iota of diplomacy. But I had in mind the whole historical road of Lenin, his whole theoretical position, his strategy, his way of building the party. This does not, however, relate to every single one of the polemical quotations which are moreover misused today for purposes alien to Leninism. In 1926, in the period of the bloc with Zinoviev, Radek warned me: Zinoviev

needs my declaration that Lenin was right in order
to excuse a little his, Zinoviev's, wrong against me.
Naturally, I understood this well. And that is why
I said at the Seventh Plenum of the E. C. C. I. that
I meant the historical right of Lenin and his party,
but in no case the right of my present critics who
strive to cover themselves with quotations plucked out
of Lenin.

Today, I am unfortunately compelled to extend
these words to Radek. With regard to the permanent revolution, I spoke only of the *defects* of the
theory, which were inevitable in so far as it was a
question of a *prognosis*. At the Seventh Plenum of
the E. C. C. I., Bucharin rightly emphasized that
Trotsky did not renounce the conception in its entirety. On the "defects", I shall speak in another,
more extensive work, in which I shall endeavor to present the experiences of the three revolutions and their
application to the further course of the Comintern, especially in the East. But in order to leave no room
for ambiguities, I wish to say here briefly: despite all
its defects, the theory of the permanent revolution,
even in the presentation of my earliest works, primarily in *Results and Perspectives* (1906) is permeated
to an incomparably greater degree with the spirit of
Marxism and consequently stands infinitely closer to
the historical line of Lenin and the Bolshevik party,
than not only the present Stalinist and Bucharinist
retrospective wisdom but also than the latest work of
Radek. By this, however, I do not at all want to say
that the conception of the revolution presents the same
immovable line in all my writings. I have not occupied
myself with the collection of old quotations—I am
forced to do it now by the period of party reaction
and epigonism—but I have plainly and honestly sought

to analyze the real processes of life. In the twelve
years (1905-1917) of my revolutionary journalistic
activity, there are also articles in which the conjunctural relations and even the conjunctural polemical
exaggerations inevitable in struggle, stand out in violation of the strategic line. Thus, for example, articles can be found in which I expressed doubts about
the future revolutionary rôle of the peasantry as a
whole, as a group, and in connection with this refused
to characterize, especially during the imperialist war,
the future Russian revolution as "national", for I felt
this characterization to be ambiguous. But it must
not be forgotten here that the historical processes that
interest us, also in the peasantry, are far more obvious
now that they have been accomplished than in those
days when they were first developing. I would observe
in passing that Lenin, who never for a moment lost
sight of the peasant question in all its gigantic, historical magnitude and from whom we all learned this--
considered it uncertain even after the February revolution that we would succeed in tearing the peasantry
away from the bourgeoisie and linking it with the
proletariat. I might, morever, say quite in general
to my harsh critics that it is far easier to dig out in
one hour the formal contradictions in a quarter of a
century of another's newspaper articles, than it is to
preserve, oneself, if even for a year, the unity of principled line.

There remains but to mention in these introductory
lines, an especially noteworthy supplement: had the
theory of the permanent revolution been correct—says
Radek—Trotsky would have assembled a large faction
on that basis. But that did not happen. Consequently . . . the theory was false.

The argument of Radek, taken as a whole, does

not contain a trace of dialectics. One could conclude
from it that the standpoint of the Opposition on the
Chinese revolution, or the attitude of Marx in British
affairs, was false; that the position of the Comintern
with regard to the reformists in America, in Austria
and—if you wish—in all countries, is false. If
Radek's argument is taken not in its general "histor-
ico-philosophical" form, but only as applied to the
question that interests us, then it hits Radek himself;
the argument might have meaning had I been of the
opinion or, what is still more important, had events
shown, that the line of Bolshevism is in *conflict* with
it, and deviates from it ever further: only then would
there be the ground for two factions. But that is
just what Radek wants to prove. I prove, on the
contrary, that in spite of all the factional polemical
exaggerations and conjunctural accentuations of the
question, the basic strategical lines were alike. Where
should a second faction have come from? In reality,
it turned out that I worked hand in hand with the
Bolsheviks in the first revolution and later defended
this common work in the international press against
the renegades' criticism of the Mensheviks. In the
1917 revolution, I fought together with Lenin against
the democratic opportunism of those "old Bolsheviks"
who have today been elevated by the reactionary wave
and fitted for the hunt against the permanent revolution.

Finally, I never endeavored to create a grouping
on the basis of the theory of the permanent revolution. My inner-party stand was a *conciliatory* one
and when at certain moments I strove for groupings,
then it was precisely on this basis. My conciliationism was derived from a certain Social Revolutionary
fatalism. I believed that the logic of the class strug-

gle would compel both factions to pursue the same revolutionary line. The great historical significance of
Lenin's stand was still unclear to me at that time, his
policy of irreconcilable ideological demarcation and,
when necessary, split, for the purpose of uniting and
steeling the backbone of the truly revolutionary party.
In 1911, Lenin wrote on this subject:

"Conciliationism is the result of moods, endeavors
and opinions which are inseparably bound up with the
nature of the historical task put before the Russian
Social Democratic Party in the counter-revolutionary
epochs of 1908-1911. That is why a whole series of
social democrats deteriorated into conciliationism in
this epoch, *proceeding from the most variegated premises.* Conciliationism was represented most consistently by Trotsky who, almost alone, endeavored to
lay a theoretical foundation for this current." (Volume XI, part 2, page 371.)

By striving for unity at all costs, I involuntarily
and unavoidably had to idealize the Centrist tendencies
in Menshevism. Despite the threefold episodic attempts, I arrived at no common work with the Mensheviks, and I could not arrive at it. Simultaneously,
however, the conciliatory line brought me into an all
the harsher position towards Bolshevism, since Lenin,
in contrast to the Mensheviks, mercilessly rejected conciliationism, and could do no different. It is obvious
that no faction could be created on the platform of
conciliationism. Thence the lesson: it is inadmissible
and harmful to bend back or weaken a political line
in favor of vulgar conciliationism; it is inadmissible
to gloss over Centrism zig-zagging to the Left; it is
inadmissible, in the hunt after the will-o'-the-wisps of
Centrism, to exaggerate differences of opinion with
genuine revolutionary co-thinkers. These are the real

lessons of Trotsky's mistakes. These lessons are very
significant. They preserve their full force even today
and it is precisely Radek who should meditate well
upon them.

* * *

With the cynicism that marks him out, Stalin once
said:

"Trotsky must know that Lenin fought to the end
of his life against the theory of the permanent revolution. But this does not disturb him." (PRAVDA, No.
261, November 12, 1926.)

This is a rude, disloyal, that is, a purely Stalinist
caricature of reality. In an appeal to the foreign
Communists, Lenin declared that differences of opinion among the Communists are something quite different from differences of opinion with the social democrats. Such differences of opinion, he wrote, Bolshevism had already gone through before. But

" . . . at the moment of the capture of power and
the creation of the Soviet republic, Bolshevism was
united and drew to it the best of the currents of socialist thought closest to it." (Vol. XVI, page 333.)

What closest currents of socialist thought did Lenin
have in mind when he wrote these lines? Martinov or
Kuusinen? Or Cachin, Thälmann and Smeral? Did
they perhaps appear to him as the "best" of the closest currents? What other tendency was closer to
Bolshevism than the one which I represented in all the
questions of principle, including the peasant question?
Even Rosa Luxemburg shrank back at first from the
agrarian policy of the Bolshevik government. For
me, however, there was no question about it at all.
We were together at the table when Lenin, pencil in
hand, wrote down the draft of his agrarian law. And
the interchange of opinions hardly consisted of more

than a dozen brief rejoinders, the sense of which was about the following: a contradictory, but historically quite unavoidable step; under the régime of the proletarian dictatorship and in the extension of the world revolution, the contradictions will be adjusted—we only need time. If a diametrical antagonism existed in the peasant question between the theory of the permanent revolution and Lenin's dialectics, how then does Radek want to explain the fact that, without renouncing my fundamental views on the course of development of the revolution, I did not stumble for an instant over the peasant question in 1917, as did the majority of the Bolshevik heads at that time? How does Radek explain the fact that after the February revolution the present theoreticians and politicians of anti-Trotskyism—the Zinovievs, Kamenevs, Stalins, Molotovs, etc., etc.—adopted, to the last man, the vulgar-democratic but not proletarian position? And once more: of whom and of what could Lenin have spoken when he referred to the fusion of Bolshevism with the best elements of the Marxist currents closest to it? And does not Lenin's *conclusive* judgment on the past differences of opinion show that in any case he saw no two irreconcilable strategical lines?

Still more noteworthy in this respect is Lenin's speech in the session of the Petrograd Committee of November 1-14, 1917*. There the question was considered of an agreement with the Mensheviks and Social Revolutionists. The supporters at that time of a coalition endeavored, even there, very timidly, to be sure, to rimt at "Trotskyism". What did Lenin re-

---

* As is known, the voluminous minutes of this historic session were torn out of the jubilee book at the special command of Stalin and to this day are kept concealed from the party.

ply?

"Agreement? I cannot even speak seriously about
that. Trotsky has long ago said that unity is impossible. Trotsky has understood this—since then
there has been no better Bolshevik."

Not the permanent revolution, but conciliationism
was what separated me, according to Lenin's views,
from Bolshevism. In order to become the "best Bolshevik", I only needed, as we see, to understand the
impossibility of an agreement with the Mensheviks.

But how is the abrupt character of Radek's turn
precisely in the question of the permanent revolution
to be explained? I believe I have one element of the
explanation. In 1916, as we learn from his writings,
Radek was in agreement with the permanent revolution, but in the Bucharinist interpretation, according
to which the bourgeois revolution in Russia is termin-
ated—not only the revolutionary rôle of the bourgeoisie, and not even the historical rôle of the slogan
of the "democratic" dictatorship, but the bourgeois
revolution as such—and that the proletariat must
therefore proceed to the capture of power under a
purely socialist banner. Radek manifestly also interpreted my position at that time in the Bucharinist
manner: otherwise he could not declare his solidarity
with Bucharin and me at one and the same time. This
also explains why Lenin polemicized against Bucharin
and Radek, with whom he did work together, having
them appear under the pseudonym of Trotsky. (Radek
admits this also in his article.) I remember that also
M. N. Pokrovsky, a co-worker of Bucharin, and a
tireless constructor of historical schemata, Marxisti-
cally colored with great skill, alarmed me in Paris,
in conversations on this question, with his dubious
"solidarity". (In politics, Pokrovsky was and re-

mains an anti-Cadet, which he honestly believes to be Bolshevism.)

In 1924-1925, Radek apparently still lived upon spiritual recollections of the Bucharinist position of 1916, which he continued to identify with mine. Rightly disillusioned by the hopelessness of his position on the basis of a fleeting study of Lenin's writings, Radek, as frequently used to happen in such cases, described an arc of 180 degrees right over my head. This is very probable because it is typical. Thus Bucharin, who in 1923-1925 turned a complete somersault himself, that is, transformed himself from an ultra-Leftist into an opportunist, constantly attributes to me his own ideological past, which he palms off as "Trotskyism". In the first period of the campaign against me, when I often still managed to look over Bucharin's articles, I would frequently ask myself: where did he get this from?—but soon guessed that he had glanced into his diary of yesterday. And now I wonder if the same psychological foundation does not lie at the bottom of Radek's conversion from a Paul of the permanent revolution into its Saul. I do not presume to insist upon this hypothesis. But I can find no other explanation.

* * *

One way or the other, according to a French expression: the flask is uncorked, the wine must be drunk. We are compelled to undertake a pretty far excursion into the realm of old quotations. I have reduced their number as much as was feasible. Yet there are many of them. Let this fact serve as justification: that I strive throughout to find in the enforced rummaging among old quotations the threads to the burning questions of the present.

II

The Permanent Revolution Is Not a "Leap" of the Proletariat, but the Transformation of the Nation under the Leadership of the Proletariat

RADEK writes:

"The essential feature that distinguishes the train of thought which is called the theory and tactic [observe: tactic too—L. T.] of the 'permanent revolution' from Lenin's theory lies in *mixing up the stage of the bourgeois revolution with the stage of the socialist revolution.*"

Intimately connected with this fundamental reproach, or resulting from it, there are other, no less serious accusations: Trotsky did not understand that "under Russian conditions, a socialist revolution which does not grow out of the democratic revolution is impossible". From which results of itself the "skipping of the stage of the democratic dictatorship". Trotsky "denies" the rôle of the peasantry which is where "the community of views of Trotsky and the Mensheviks" lay. As already said, all this is to prove by the system of circumstantial evidence the incorrectness of my position in the fundamental questions of the Chinese revolution.

To be sure, in the formal literary respect, Radek can refer here and there to Lenin. And he does that: everybody has "at hand" *this* part of the quotations. But as I shall soon demonstrate, these contentions of Lenin in regard to me had a purely episodic character and were incorrect, that is, in no sense did they characterize my real position in 1905. In Lenin himself there are quite different, directly contrary and far better grounded remarks on my attitude in the principled questions of the revolution. Radek did not even make the attempt to unite the various and directly antithetical remarks of Lenin, and to elucidate these polemical contradictions by a comparison with my actual views*.

In 1906, Lenin published, with his own foreword, an article by Kautsky on the motive forces of the Russian revolution. Without knowing anything about this, I also translated Kautsky's article in prison, provided it with a foreword and included it in my book *On the Defense of the Party.* Both Lenin and I expressed our thorough accord with Kautsky's analysis. To Plechanov's question: Is our revolution bourgeois or socialist? Kautsky had answered that it is no longer

---

* I recollect that I called out to Bucharin at the Seventh Plenum of the Executive Committee of the Communist International when he cited the same quotations: "But there are also directly contrary quotations in Lenin." After a brief moment of perplexity, Bucharin retorted: "I know that, I know that, but I am taking what I need, not what you need." There is the quick repartee of this theoretician for you!

bourgeois, but not yet socialist, that is, it presents
the transitional form from the one to the other. To
this, Lenin wrote in his foreword:

"Are we confronted by a bourgeois or a socialist
revolution, in its whole character? That is the old
schema, says Kautsky. That is not how the question
should be put, that is not Marxian. The revolution
in Russia is not bourgeois, for the bourgeoisie is not
a driving force of the present revolutionary movement
of Russia. But neither is the revolution in Russia
socialist." (Volume VIII, page 82.)

Yet not a few passages can be found in Lenin, written before and after this foreword, where he categor-
ically calls the Russian revolution bourgeois. Is that
a contradiction? If Lenin is approached with the
methods of the present critics of "Trotskyism", then
dozens and hundreds of such "contradictions" can be
found, which are clarified for the serious and conscientious reader by the difference in the posing of
the question at different moments, which in no way
violates the unity of Lenin's conception.

On the other hand, I never disputed the bourgeois
character of the revolution in the sense of its actual
historical tasks, but only in the sense of its motive
forces and its perspective. My fundamental work of
those days (1905-1906) on the permanent revolution,
begins with the following sentences:

"The Russian revolution came unexpectedly to everybody but the social democracy. Marxism long ago
foretold the inevitability of the Russian revolution
which had to come as a result of the collision of the
forces of capitalist development with the forces of
inflexible absolutism. By characterizing it as bourgeois, it pointed out that the *immediate objective* tasks
of the revolution consisted of the creation of 'normal'

conditions for the development of bourgeois society as a whole. *Marxism was right.* This can no longer be disputed today, nor need it be demonstrated. The Marxists are confronted with a quite different task: by an analysis of the internal mechanics of the developing revolution to disclose its 'possibilites'.

"The Russian revolution has a quite peculiar character, which is the result of the peculiarities of our whole socio-historical evolution and which, in regard to it, opens up quite new historical perspectives." (*Our Revolution*, 1906, article *Results and Perspectives*, page 224.)

"The general sociological characterization—*bourgeois revolution*—in no way settles the politico-tactical problems, contradictions and difficulties which are raised by this *given* bourgeois revolution". (*Ibid*, page 249.)

In this way, I did not dispute the bourgeois character of the revolution that stood on the order of the day and mix up democracy and socialism. But I endeavored to show that with us the class dialectics of the bourgeois revolution would bring the proletariat to power and that without its dictatorship not even the democratic tasks could be solved. In the same article (1905-1906) it says:

"The proletariat grows and consolidates itself with the growth of capitalism. In this sense, the development of capitalism signifies the development of the proletariat toward the dictatorship. But the day and hour when the power passes into the hands of the proletariat do not depend *directly* upon the state of the productive forces, but upon the conditions of the class struggle, upon the international situation, and finally, upon a series of objective factors: tradition, initiative, readiness for struggle. . . .

"In an economically backward country, the proletariat can come to power sooner than in the economically advanced countries. The conception of some
sort of automatic dependence of the proletarian dictatorship upon the technical forces and resources of
the country constitutes an extremely over-simplified
'economic' materialism. This view has nothing in
common with Marxism.

"The Russian revolution, in our opinion, creates
such conditions under which the power can pass over
to the proletariat (and with a victorious revolution it
must) even *before* the policy of bourgeois liberalism
acquires the possibility to bring its state genius to a
full unfolding". (*Ibid*, page 245.)

These lines contain a polemic against that vulgar
"Marxism" which not only prevailed in 1905-1906 but
also gave the tone to the conference of the Bolsheviks
in March 1917 before Lenin's arrival, and found its
crassest expression in Rykov at the April conference.
At the Sixth Congress of the Comintern, this pseudo-
Marxism, that is, "common sense" debauched by
scholasticism, constituted the "scientific" basis of the
speeches of Kuusinen and many others. And this, ten
years after the October revolution!

Since I have not the possibility of describing here the
whole train of thought of *Results and Perspectives*, I
should like to adduce one more clearly expressed quotation from my article in NATCHALO (1905):

"Our liberal bourgeoisie comes forward as counter-
revolutionary even before the revolutionary climax.
In every critical moment, our intellectual democracy
only demonstrates its impotence. The peasantry in its
entirety represents an elementary rebellion. It can be
put at the service of the revolution only by the force
that takes over state power. The vanguard position

of the working class in the revolution, the direct connection between it and the revolutionary village, the
spell by which it conquers the army—all this pushes
it inevitably to power. The complete victory of the
revolution means the victory of the proletariat. This
in turn means the further uninterrupted advance of
the revolution." (*Our Revolution,* page 172.)

The perspective of the dictatorship of the proletariat consequently grows here, precisely out of the
bourgeois-democratic revolution—in contradiction to
all that Radek writes. That is just why the revolution is called permanent (uninterrupted). But the
dictatorship of the proletariat does not come after the
completion of the democratic revolution, as Radek
would have it in such a case, it would simply be impossible in Russia, for in a backward country the
numerically weak proletariat cannot attain power if
the tasks of the peasantry have been solved during the
preceding stage. No, the dictatorship of the proletariat appeared probable and even inevitable on the
basis of the bourgeois revolution precisely because
there was no other power and no other way to solve
the tasks of the agrarian revolution. But this alone
opens up the perspective of the democratic revolution
growing over into a socialist revolution.

"Entering the government not as impotent hostages,
but as the leading power, the representatives of the
proletariat already destroy by that alone the boundaries between the minimum and maximum programs,
that is, they *put collectivism on the order of the day.*
At what point on this road the proletariat will be
halted depends upon the relation of forces, but not
upon the original designs of the party of the proletariat. That is why there can also be no question of
some sort of *special* form of the proletarian dictator-

ship in the bourgeois revolution, namely, the *democrat-ic* dictatorship of the proletariat (or of the proletariat and peasantry). The working class cannot assure the democratic character of its dictatorship without over-stepping the boundaries of its democratic program.

"If the party of the proletariat takes over power, it will fight for this power to the end. If one of the means of this struggle for the maintenance and con-solidation of the power is agitation and organization especially in the village, then the other means will con-sist of the collectivist program. Collectivism will not only be the inevitable consequence of the fact that the party is in power but also the means of insuring this situation based on the proletariat." (*Results and Perspectives*, page 258.)

Let us go further:

"We know the classic example [I wrote in 1908 against the Menshevik, Tcherevanin] of a revolution in which the conditions for the rule of the capitalist bour-geoisie were prepared by the terrorist dictatorship of the victorious *sansculottes*. That was in an epoch when the principal mass of the urban population was composed of artisans and tradesmen, that is, of the petty bourgeoisie. It followed the leadership of the Jacobins. The principal mass of the urban popula-tion in Russia is composed today of the industrial proletariat. This analogy alone points to the possi-bility of such an historical situation in which the vic-tory of the 'bourgeois' revolution is granted only by the conquest of revolutionary power by the proletar-iat. Does the revolution thereby cease to be bour-geois? Yes and no. This does not depend upon the formal designation, but upon the further development of events. If the proletariat is overthrown by the coalition parties, among them also the peasantry it liberated, then the revolution retains its limited bourgeois character. Should the proletariat, however, find it possible to set in motion all the means of its political rule in order to break through the national limits of the Russian revolution, then it can become the prologue to the socialist world era. The question: What stage will the Russian revolution attain? permits naturally only a conditioned reply. Only one thing is absolutely and indubitably correct: the naked characterization of the Russian revolution as *bourgeois* tells us nothing about the type of its internal development and in no case signifies that the proletariat must adopt its tactic to the conduct of the bourgeois democracy as the only legal claimant to state power." (L. Trotsky, *1905*, page 263, Russian edition.)

From the same article:

"Our revolution, which is a bourgeois revolution according to the immediate tasks it grew out of, knows, as a consequence of the extreme class differentiation of the industrial population, of no bourgeois class which could place itself at the head of the popular masses by combining its social weight and political experience with revolutionary energy. *The suppressed worker and peasant masses, left to their own resources, must take it upon themselves to create,* in the hard school of implacable conflict and cruel defeat, *the necessary political and organizational preconditions for their triumph.* No other road is open to them." (L. Trotsky, *1905*, pages 267-8.)

One more quotation from *Results and Perspectives* on the most violently assailed point—on the peasantry —must be adduced. In the special chapter *The Proletariat in Power and the Peasantry*, the following is said:

"The proletariat will not be able to insure its power

without broadening the base of its revolution.

"Many sections of the toiling masses, especially in the village, will be drawn into the revolution and embraced by a political organization for the first time, only after the vanguard of the revolution, the city proletariat, has placed itself at the helm of state power. Revolutionary agitation and organization will be carried out with the help of state resources. Finally, the legislative power itself will become a mighty instrument for revolutionizing the masses of the people. . . .

"The fate of the most elementary interests of the peasantry—even of the *whole peasantry* as a *class*— is knit togther with the fate of the revolution, i. e., with the fate of the proletariat.

"*The proletariat in power will appear to the peasantry as the liberating class.*

"The rule of the proletariat will not only mean: democratic equality, free self-administration, transference of the tax burden to the possessing classes, transformation of the standing army into the armed people, abolition of compulsory church taxes, but also recognition of all the revolutionary redivisions (seizures) of landed property undertaken by the peasantry. The proletariat will make this redivision the point of departure for further state measures in the field of agriculture. Under these conditions, the Russian peasantry in the first, most difficult period will be no less interested in supporting the proletarian régime than the French peasantry in supporting the military régime of Napoleon Bonaparte, which guaranteed the new possessors the inviolability of their land tracts by virtue of the bayonet. . . .

"But perhaps the peasantry will dislodge the proletariat and itself occupy its place?

"This is impossible. All historical experience pro-
tests against such an assumption. This experience
proves that the peasantry is entirely incapable of an
independent political rôle." (Page 251.)

All this was written not in 1929, nor yet in 1924,
but in 1905. Does this look like "ignoring the peasantry", I should like to know? Where is the "jumping over" the agrarian question here? Is it not time,
friends, to show somewhat more of a sense of propriety?

Now let us see in what condition this "sense of
propriety" is with Stalin. Referring to my New York
articles on the February 1917 revolution, which agree
in every essential with Lenin's Geneva articles, the
theoretician of party reaction writes:

"The letters of comrade Trotsky, both in spirit and
in conclusions, are entirely dissimilar from Lenin's
letters, for they repeat entirely the anti-Bolshevik
slogan of Trotsky: 'No czar—and a labor government', a slogan which means: Revolution without the
peasantry." (Speech to the fraction of the Central
Committee of the Trade Unions, November 19, 1924.)

Exquisite is the sound of these words on the "anti-
Bolshevik slogan" (allegedly Trotsky's): "No czar—
and a labor government." According to Stalin, the
Bolshevik slogan should have read: "No labor government, but a czar." We will still speak of the alleged
"slogan" of Trotsky. But we would first like to hear
from another of the notables of the ruling spirit of
the day, less illiterate perhaps, but one who has, however, taken leave forever from any theoretical scruples:
I speak of Lunatcharsky:

"In 1905, Leo Davidovitch Trotsky inclined to the
idea: *the proletariat must remain isolated* [!] and
must not support the bourgeoisie, for that would be

opportunism; for the proletariat alone, however,
it would be very difficult to carry through the
revolution, because the proletariat at that time
amounted to only seven-eighths of a percent of the
total population and no great war could be conducted
with so small a cadre. Thus, Leo Davidovitch decided that the proletariat in Russia must support the
permanent revolution, that is, fight for the greatest
possible success, until the fiery sparks of this con-
flagration blew the powder deposits of the world
into the air." (THE POWER OF THE SOVIETS, No. 7,
On the Characteristics of the October Revolution, by
A. Lunatcharsky, page 10.)

The proletariat "must remain isolated" until the
fiery sparks blow up the powder deposits . . . How
beautifully many People's Commissars write who are
for the moment not yet "isolated" in spite of the
threatened position of their own mental power*. But
we do not want to be so severe with Lunatcharsky:
from each according to his abilities. His slovenly
absurdities are no more senseless than those of many
others.

But how, according to Trotsky, must "the proletariat remain isolated"? Let us adduce one quotation
from my polemic against Struve (1906). At the time,
Lunatcharsky chanted immoderate hymns of praise for
this work. While the bourgeois parties—the reference is to the Soviet of Deputies—"remained entirely
aloof" from the awakening masses.

" . . . political life became concentrated around
the workers' Soviet. The attitude of the city masses

---

* Since this was written, Lunatcharsky has been "isolated"
and his place as Commissar of Education given to Bubnov.
—Tr.

to the Soviet (1905) was manifestly sympathetic, even if not clear. All the oppressed and offended sought its protection. The popularity of the Soviet grew far beyond the city. It received 'petitions' from peasants who suffered injustices, peasants' resolutions poured into the Soviet, delegations from village communities came to it. Here, right here is where were concentrated the thoughts and sympathies of the nation, of the real and not the falsified democratic nation." (*Our Revolution*, page 199.)

In all these quotations—their number can easily be increased two-, three-, and tenfold—the permanent revolution is described as a revolution which welds together the oppressed masses of city and village around the proletariat organized in Soviets; as a national revolution that raises the proletariat to power and by that alone affords the possibility of the democratic revolution growing into a socialist revolution.

The permanent revoluton is no isolated leap of the proletariat, rather it is the rebuilding of the whole nation under the leadership of the proletariat. That is how I pictured the perspective of the permanent revolution since 1905, and so I construed it.

*   *   *

Radek is also wrong with regard to Parvus*— whose views on the Russian revolution in 1905 bordered closely on mine, without, however, being identical with them—when he repeats the stereotyped phrase about Parvus' "leap" from the czarist to the social democratic government. Radek actually refutes himself when, in another part of his article, he indicates in passing but quite correctly, *wherein* my views on

---

* It should be remembered that at that time Parvus stood at the extreme Left wing of international Marxism.

the revolution actually differed from those of Parvus.
Parvus was not of the opinion that the labor government in Russia has a way out in the direction of the
socialist revolution, that is, that in the process of
fulfilling the tasks of democracy it can emerge into
the socialist dictatorship. As is proved by the quotation from 1905 adduced by Radek himself, Parvus
confined the tasks of the labor government to the tasks
of *democracy*.   Then where is the leap to *socialism?*
As a result of the revolutionary overthrow, the erection of a labor government on the "Australian" model
already then hovered before Parvus.   Parvus also
made the comparison between Russia and Australia
after the October revolution, when he himself already
stood at the extreme Right wing of social reformism.
Bucharin said about this that Parvus had "discovered"
Australia after the fact in order to cover up his old
sins with regard to the permanent revolution.   But
that is wrong.   In 1905, Parvus saw in the conquest
of power by the proletariat the road to democracy
and not to socialism, that is, he asssigned to the proletariat only that rôle which it actually played in
Russia in the first eight to ten months of the October
revolution.   As a further perspective, Parvus even
then pointed to the Australian democracy of that
time, that is, to a régime in which the labor party
does indeed govern but does not rule, and carries out
its reformist demands only as the supplement to the
program of the bourgeoisie.   Irony of fate: the fundamental tendency of the Right-Centrist bloc of 1923-
1928 consisted precisely of drawing the dictatorship
of the proletariat closer to the labor democracy of
the Australian model, that is, of the prognosis of Parvus.   This becomes all the clearer when it is recalled
that the Russian philistine "socialists" of two or three

decades ago continually depicted Australia in the Russian press as a workers' and peasants' country which, shut off from the outer world by high tariffs, was developing "socialist" legislation and in that way was building socialism in one country. Radek would have acted correctly had he pushed *this* side of the question to the foreground instead of repeating the fairy tales of the fantastic skipping over of democracy.

IIII

Three Elements of the "Democratic Dictatorship":

Classes, Tasks and Political Mechanics

---

*T*HE DIFFERENCE between the "permanent" standpoint and that of Lenin, expressed itself politically
in the contrast of the slogan of the dictatorship of the
proletariat which supports itself upon the peasantry
and the slogan of the *democratic* dictatorship of the
proletariat and the peasantry. The dispute was not
concerned with whether the bourgeois-democratic stage
could be skipped and whether an alliance between the
workers and the peasants was necessary—it concerned
the *political mechanics* of the collaboration of the proletariat and the peasantry in the democratic revolution.

Far too presumptive, not to say light-minded, is
Radek's contention that only people "who have not
thought out the complexity of the methods of Marxism
and Leninism to the end" could push to the foreground
the question of the *party-political expression* of the
democratic dictatorship, when Lenin saw the whole
question only in the collaboration of the two classess
in the objective historical task. No, that is not how
it stood.

If the subjective factor of the revolution, the parties and their programs—in this case, the political and organizational form of the collaboration of proletariat and peasantry — is abandoned, then there vanish all the differences of opinion, not only between Lenin and me, which marked two shades of the same revolutionary wing, but what is certainly worse, also the differences of opinion between Bolshevism and Menshevism, and finally, the differences between the Russian revolution of 1905 and the revolutions of 1848 and even of 1789, in so far as the proletariat can at all be spoken of in relation to the latter. *All* bourgeois revolutions have rested on the cooperation of the oppressed classes of city and country. That is just what invested the revolutions to a lesser or greater degree with a national character, that is, one embracing the whole people.

The theoretical as well as the political dispute among us was not over the collaboration of the worker and peasant as such, but over the program of this collaboration, its party forms and political methods. In the old revolutions, workers and peasants "collaborated" under the leadership of the liberal bourgeoisie or its petty bourgeois democratic wing. The Communist International repeated the experiment of the *old* revolutions in a *new* historical situation by doing everything it could to subject the Chinese workers and peasants to the political leadership of the national liberal Chiang Kai-Shek and later, of the "democrat" Wang Chin Wei. Lenin put the question of an alliance of the workers and peasants in irreconcilable antagonism to the liberal bougeoisie. Such an alliance had never existed in history before. It was a matter, so far as its method went, of a new experiment in the collaboration of the oppressed class of

city and village. By this, the question of the political forms of the collaboration was posed for the first
time. Radek has simply overlooked this. That is
why he leads us back not only from the formula of the
permanent revolution, but also from Lenin's "democratic dictatorship" into the vacuum of historical ab-
stractions. Yes, Lenin refused for a number of years
to *answer in advance* the question of what the political
party and state organization of the democratic dictatorship of the proletariat and the peasantry would look
like and he pushed into the foreground the collaboration of these two classes in contrast to the coalition
with the liberal bourgeoisie. Lenin said: At a certain
historical stage, there inevitably results from the whole
objective situation the revolutionary alliance of the
working class with the peasantry for the solution of
the tasks of the democratic revolution. Whether the
peasantry will have time enough or will understand how
to create a party of its own, whether this party will
be the specific gravity of the representatives of the
proletariat in the revolutionary government—all these
questions permit of no generally valid reply. "Experience will show!" Even though the formula of the
democratic dictatorship left open the question of the
political mechanics of the alliance of the workers and
peasants, it nevertheless remained, up to a certain
period, without being converted into a naked abstraction like Radek's, an algebraic formula which allowed of greatly divergent political constructions for
the future.

Lenin himsef was in no way of the opinion that the
question would be exhausted by the class basis of the
dictatorship and its objective historical aim. The
significance of the subjective factors: of the aim, the
conscious method, the party—Lenin well understood

and taught all this to us. And that is why Lenin, in his commentaries to his slogan, did not renounce even a hypothetical reply to the question: what political forms might be assumed by the first independent alliance of workers and peasants in history. However, Lenin took up the question differently at different times. Lenin's ideas must not be regarded dogmatically. Lenin brought no finished comments from Sinai, but forged ideas and slogans in the furnace of the class struggle. He adapted these slogans to reality, making them concrete and precise, and at different times filled them with different content. But *this side* of the question, which later gained a decisive character, and brought the Bolshevik party right to the verge of a split at the beginning of 1917, has not been studied by Radek; he simply ignored it.

It is, however, a fact that Lenin did not always characterize the probable party-political expression and governmental form of the alliance of the two classes in the same way and that he refrained from binding the party by hypothetical interpretations, What are the reasons for such caution? The reasons are to be sought in the fact that one element of this algebraic formula is represented by a quantity, gigantic in significance, but politically extremely indefinite: *the peasantry.*

I want to quote only a few examples of Lenin's interpretation of the democratic dictatorship, observing, however, that a cohesive characterization of the *evolution* of Lenin's idea in this question would require a separate work.

Developing the thought that the proletariat and the peasantry would be the basis of the dictatorship, Lenin wrote in March 1905:

"And this composition of the social basis of the

probable and desirable revolutionary dictatorship will
naturally also be expressed in the composition of the
revolutionary government, *it will render inevitable the
participation of the most varied representatives of the
revolutionary democracy in this government and even
their predominance.*" (Volume VI, Russian edition,
page 132.   My emphasis.)

In these words, Lenin shows not only the class basis
but also a definite governmental form of the dictatorship with a possible predominance of the representatives of the petty bourgeois democracy.

In 1907, Lenin wrote:

"The peasant agrarian revolution of which you
speak, gentlemen, must, in order to triumph as such, as
a peasant revolution, become the central power of the
whole state."   (Volume IX, page 539.)

This formula goes even further.   It can be understood in the sense that the revolutionary power must
be directly concentrated in the hands of the peasantry.   This   formula,   however,   also embraces, in the
more far-reaching interpretation accorded it by the
passage of developments, the October revolution which
brought the proletariat to power as the "agent" of the
peasant revolution.   These are the extreme poles of
the permissible interpretations of the formula of the
democratic dictatorship of the proletariat and the
peasantry.   It is probable that—up to a certain point
—its strength lay in this algebraic instability, but
its dangers also lay there, manifested themselves among
us crassly enough in February and led to the catas-
trophe in China.

In July 1905, Lenin wrote:

"Nobody speaks of the seizure of power by the
party—we speak only of participation, as leading a
participation in the revolution *as possible.* . . . " (Vol-

ume VI, page 228.)

In December 1906, Lenin considered it possible to agree with Kautsky in the question of the seizure of power by the party:

"Kautsky considers it not only 'as very probable' that 'victory will fall to the social democratic party in the course of the revolution,' but declares it the duty of the social democrats 'to suggest the certainty of victory to their adherents, for one cannot fight successfully if victory is renounced beforehand.'" (Volume VIII, page 58.)

The distance between these two interpretations given by Lenin himself is no smaller than between Lenin's formulations and mine. We will see this even more plainly later on. Here we want to raise the question: What is the meaning of these contradictions in Lenin? They reflect the same great unknown in the political formula of the revolution: *the peasantry.* Not for nothing did the radicals once call the peasant the Sphinx of Russian history. The question of the nature of the revolutionary dictatorship—whether Radek wills it or not—is inseparable from the question of the possibility of a revolutionary peasant party hostile to the liberal bourgeoisie and independent of the proletariat. Were the peasantry capable of creating an *independent* party in the epoch of the democratic revolution then the democratic revolution could be realized in its truest and most direct sense, and the question of the participation of the proletarian minority would obtain an important, it is true, but subordinated significance. The matter presents itself quite differently if one proceeds from the fact that the peasantry, because of its hybrid class character and the lack of uniformity of its social composition, can have neither an independent policy nor an independent party, and is compelled, in the revolutionary epoch, to choose between the policy of the bourgeoisie and the policy of the proletariat. Only this evaluation of the political nature of the peasantry produces the perspective of the dictatorship of the proletariat which grows directly out of the democratic revolution. In this, naturally, there lies no "denial", "ignoring" or "underestimation" of the peasantry. Without the decisive significance of the agrarian question for the life of all society and without the deep and gigantic impulsion of the peasant revolution there could in general be no talk about the proletarian dictatorship in Russia. But the fact that the *agrarian revolution* created the conditions for the dictatorship of the *proletariat* grew out of the inability of the peasantry to solve its own historical problem with its own resources and under its own leadership. Under present conditions in bourgeois countries, even in the backward ones, in so far as they have already entered the epoch of capitalist industry and are bound into a unit by railroads and telegraphs—this refers not only to Russia, but to China and India as well—the peasantry is still less capable of a leading or even only an independent political rôle than in the epoch of the old bourgeois revolutions. Because I constantly and persistently underlined this idea, which forms one of the most important constituents of the theory of the permanent revolution, was a completely insufficient and, in essence, quite unfounded reason for accusing me of an underestimation of the peasantry.

How does Lenin stand on the question of a peasant party? To reply to this question, a special article would have to be devoted to the transformation of Lenin's views on the Russian revolution in the period of 1905-1917. Let us confine ourselves here to two quotations.

In 1907, Lenin wrote:

"It is possible . . . that the objective difficulties of a unification of the petty bourgeoisie will check the formation of such a party and leave the peasant democracy for a long time in the present state of a spongy, shapeless, pulpy, Trudovik-like* mass." (Volume VIII, page 494.)

In 1909, Lenin expressed himself on the same theme as follows:

"There is not the slightest doubt that a revolution which reaches so high a degree of development as the revolutionary dictatorship, will create a more firmly formed and more powerful revolutionary peasant party. To judge the matter otherwise would mean to assume that in a grown-up man, the size, form and degree of development of certain essential organs could remain in an embryonic state." (Volume XI, Part 1, page 230.)

Was this assumption confirmed? No, it was not. But that is just what induced Lenin, *up to the moment of the complete historical verification,* to give only a conditioned reply to the question of the revolutionary power. It is self-understood that Lenin did not put his hypothetical formula above the reality. The struggle for the independent political party of the proletariat constituted the main content of his life. The woeful epigones, however, in the hunt after a peasants' party, landed at the subordination of the Chinese workers to the Kuo Min Tang, at the strangulation of Communism in India in the name of the "Workers' and

---

* The Trudoviki were the representatives of the peasants in the four Dumas, constantly oscillating between the Cadets [Liberals] and the social democrats.

Peasants' Party", at the dangerous fiction of the Peasant's International, at the masquerade of the Anti-Imperialist League, and so on.

Prevailing thought at present makes no effort to dwell on the contradictions in Lenin adduced above, which exist in part externally and in appearance, in part also in reality, but which always result from the problem itself. Ever since we have had a special species of "Red" professors, who are frequently distinguished from the old reactionary professors not by a firmer backbone but by a profounder illiteracy, Lenin is now professorially trimmed and purged of all contradictions, that is, of the dynamics of his thought; standard quotations are threaded on a few thin strings, and then, according to the requirements of the "given moment", set in circulation serially.

It must not be forgotten for a moment that the problems of the revolution in a politically "virgin" country became acute after a great historical interval, after a lengthy reactionary epoch in Europe and in the whole world, and by that alone already brought with them much that was obscure. In the formula "democratic dictatorship of the workers and peasants", Lenin gave expression to the specific social relationships in Russia. He put different constructions upon this formula, but never rejected it without having exhaustively measured the peculiarity in the conditions of the Russian revolution. Wherein lay this peculiarity?

The gigantic rôle of the agrarian question and the peasant question in general, as the basis or substructure of all other problems, and the great number of the peasant *intelligenzia* and those who sympathized with the peasant, with their populist ideology, the "anticapitalist" traditions and the revolutionary tempering—all this in its entirety signified that if *an anti-bourgeois revolutionary peasant party was at all possible anywhere, then it was precisely and primarily in Russia.*

And as a matter of fact, out of the endeavor to create a peasant, or a worker and peasant—in distinction from a liberal and proletarian—party, every possible variation was attempted, illegal and parlia- mentary as well as their combination: *"Zemlia i Volia"* [Land and Freedom], *"Narodnaia Volia"* [People's Will], *"Tchorny Perediel"* [Black Reconstruction], the legal *"Narodnitchestvo"* [Populism], "People's So- cialists", *"Trudoviks"*, "Social Revolutionists", "Left Social Revolutionists", etc., etc. For half a century, we had, as it were, a huge laboratory for the creation of an "anti-capitalist" peasant party with an indepen- dent position towards the proletarian party. The largest size, as is known, was attained by the experi- ment of the S. R. party, which, for a time in 1917, actually constituted the party of the overwhelming majority of the peasantry. And then? It used its position only to betray the peasants completely to the liberal bourgeoisie. The S. R.s entered a coalition with the imperialists of the Entente and together with them conducted an armed struggle against the Russian proletariat.

This truly classic example shows that petty bour- geois parties on a peasant basis, even in everyday history, can maintain the appearance of an indepen- dent policy when secondary questions are on the agenda, but that when the revolutionary crisis of so- ciety puts the fundamental questions of property on the order of the day, the petty bourgeois "peasant" party automatically becomes an instrument of the bourgeoisie against the proletariat.

If my old differences of opinion with Lenin are considered not from the cross-section of quotations torn out of this and that year, month and day, but in their correct historical perspective, then it becomes quite clear that the dispute, at least on my part, was not over whether democratic tasks stand before Russia which require a revolutionary solution; not over whether an alliance of the proletariat with the peasants is required for the solution of these tasks, but over what party-political and state form the revolutionary cooperation of the proletariat and the peasantry could assume, and what consequences result from it for the further development of the revolution. I speak of course of *my* position in this dispute, not of the position of Bucharin-Radek of that time, for which they themselves must answer.

How close the formula of the "permanent revolution" approached Lenin's formula is graphically illustrated by the following comparison. In 1905, that is, before the October strike and before the December uprising in Moscow, I wrote in the foreword to one of Lassalle's speeches:

"It is self-understand that the proletariat, as in its time the bourgeoisie, fulfills its mission supported upon the peasantry and the petty bourgeoisie. The proletariat leads the village, draws it into the movement, interests it in the success of its plans. The proletariat, however, absolutely remains the leader. This is not the 'dictatorship of the peasantry and proletariat' but *the dictatorship of the proletariat supported by the peasantry*.*" (L. Trotsky, *1905,* page 281.)

---

* This quotation, together with a hundred others, shows in passing that I recognized the existence of the peasantry and

Now compare these words, written in 1905, and quoted by me in the Polish article of 1909, with the following words of Lenin, written in 1909, right after the party conference, under the pressure of Rosa Luxemburg, had adopted the formula "dictatorship of the proletariat supported by the peasantry" instead of the old Bolshevik formula. To the Mensheviks, who spoke of the radical change of Lenin's position, he replied:

" . . . The formula which the Bolsheviks have chosen for themselves here reads: '*the proletariat which leads the peasantry*'*.

" . . . Is it not obvious that the idea of all these formulations is the same? That this idea expresses precisely the dictatorship of the proletariat and peasantry, that the '*formula*'—*proletariat supported by the peasantry—remains entirely within the bounds of that very dictatorship of the proletariat and peasantry?*" (Volume XI, Part 1, pages 219 and 224. My emphasis.)

Thus Lenin puts a construction on the "algebraic" formula here which excludes the idea of an *independent* peasant party and even more of its dominant rôle in the revolutionary government: the proletariat *leads*

the significance of the agrarian question already on the eve of the 1905 revolution, that is, that I began to be aware of the significance of the peasantry somewhat earlier than the Maslows, Thalheimers, Thälmanns, Remmeles, Cachins, Monmousseaus, Bela Kuns, Peppers, Kuusinens and other Marxian sociologists.

* At the 1909 conference, Lenin recommended the formula of "the proletariat which leads the peasantry", but then he associated himself with the formula of the Polish social democrats which thereby obtained the majority at the conference against the Mensheviks.

the peasantry, the proletariat *is supported* by the peasantry, consequently the revolutionary power is concentrated into the hands of the party of the proletariat. But that is just what the central point of the permanent revolution consisted of.

The utmost that can be said today, that is, *after* the historical verification of the old differences of opinion on the question of the dictatorship, is the following: while Lenin, always proceeding from the leading rôle of the proletariat, emphasizes in every way, clears up and teaches us the necessity of the revolutionary collaboration of the workers and peasants, I, likewise always proceeding from this collaboration, emphasize in every way the necessity of proletarian leadership, not only in the bloc but also in the government which will be assembed to incorporate this bloc. No other difference can be read into the matter.

*   *   *

In connection with what has been adduced above, we would like to examine two quotations: one out of *Results and Perspectives,* which Stalin and Zinoviev utilized to prove the antagonism between my views and Lenin's, the other out of a polemical article by Lenin against me, which Radek employs for the same purpose.

Here is the first question:

"The participation of the proletariat in the government is objectively most probable and admissible in principle only as a dominant and leading participation. Naturally, this government can be called the dictatorship of the proletariat and peasantry, dictatorship of the proletariat, peasantry and *intelligenzia,* or finally, coalition government of the working class and the petty bourgeoisie. But the question still remains:

to whom does the hegemony belong in the government, and through it, in the country? If we speak of a labor government, then by that alone we already answer that the hegemony will belong to the working class." (*Our Revolution,* 1906, page 250.)

Zinoviev (in 1925) beat the drums mightily because (in 1905!) I had juxtaposed the peasantry and the *intelligenzia;* the Mensheviks, as I wrote at that time, clutched at the heels of every radical intellectual in order to prove over and over again the blossoming of bourgeois democracy. I expressed myself hundreds of times in those days on the impotence of the intellectuals as an "independent" social group and on the decisive significance of the revolutionary peasantry. Moreover, it is certainly not a question of a single polemical sentence which I have no intention at all of defending. The heart of the quotation consists of the fact that I completely accept the Leninist content of the democratic dictatorship and only demand a more precise definition of its political mechanism, that is, the rejection of a coalition in which the proletariat would only be a hostage under a petty bourgeois majority.

Now let us examine Lenin's 1906 article which, as Radek himself remarks, was directed "*formally* against Trotsky, but in *reality* against Bucharin, Piatakov, the writer of these lines [that is, Radek] and a number of other comrades." This is a very valuable affirmation which entirely confirms my impression of that time that Lenin was directing the polemic against me only in appearance, for the contents, as I shall demonstrate forthwith, did not in reality at all refer to me. The article contains (in two lines) that very accusation concerning my alleged "negation of the peasantry" which later became the main sermon of the

epigones and their disciples. The "nail" of this article—as Radek expresses it—is the following passage:

"Trotsky has not taken into consideration," says
Lenin, quoting my words, "that this is just what the
completion of the 'national bourgeois revolution' in
Russia will be when the proletariat pulls along the
non-proletarian masses of the village to the confiscation of the manorial land, and overthrows the monarchy, that this is just what *the revolutionary democratic dictatorship of the proletariat and the peasantry will be.*" (Lenin, Volume XIII, page 214.)

That Lenin did not turn to the "right address" with
the accusation of the "negation" of the peasantry, but
really meant Bucharin and Radek, who actually
wanted to skip over the democratic stage of the revolution, is clear not only from everything that has been
said above, but also from the quotation adduced by
Radek himself, which he rightly calls the "nail" of
Lenin's article. In actuality, *Lenin refers directly to
the words of my article, according to which only an
independent and bold policy of the proletariat can pull
along the "non-proletarian" masses of the village to the
confiscation of the manorial land, to the overthrow of
the monarchy,* etc., and Lenin adds: "Trotsky has not
taken into consideration that . . . this is just what
the revolutionary democratic dictatorship will be." In
other words, Lenin confirms here and, so to speak, cer-
tifies that Trotsky in reality accepts the whole genuine content of the Bolshevik formula (the collaboration
of the workers and the peasants and the democratic
tasks of this collaboration), but does not want to acknowledge that this is just what the democratic dictatorship, the completion of the national revolution,
will be. In this manner, the dispute in the apparently
"sharp" polemical article is not concerned with the

program of the next stage of the revolution and its motive class forces, but precisely with the political *relationship of these forces* to each other, with *the political and party organizational character of the dictatorship.* If, as a result of the unclarity of the process itself on the one hand, and of factional exaggeration on the other, polemical misunderstandings were comprehensible and unavoidable in *those* days, it is completely incomprehensible how Radek was able subsequently to introduce such confusion into the question.

My polemic with Lenin was concerned in essence with the possibility of the independence (and the *degree* of independence) of the peasantry in the revolution, as well as with the possibility of an independent peasants' party. In this polemic, I accused Lenin of overestimating the *independent* rôle of the peasantry. Lenin accused me of underestimating the *revolutionary* rôle of the peasantry. This resulted from the logic of the polemic itself. What but contempt, however, does one deserve who today, two decades later, tears these old quotations out of the foundation of the then party relationships, endows every polemical exaggeration and every episodic error with an absolute value, instead of revealing in the light of the greatest revolutionary experience what the actual kernel of the differences of opinion was and what the relations looked like, not on paper, but in reality.

Compelled to limit myself in the selection of quotations, I want to point here only to the comprehensive theses of Lenin on the stages of the revolution, which were written at the end of 1905, and only published for the first time in 1926 in the fifth volume of his selected works (page 451). Let us recall the fact that all the Oppositionists, Radek included, regarded

the publication of these theses as the handsomest gift
to the Opposition, for Lenin shows himself guilty of
"Trotskyism" in it. The most important points of the
resolution of the Seventh Plenum of the E. C. C. I.
which condemns Trotskyism, appear, as it were, to be
deliberately directed against the fundamental theses of
Lenin. The Stalinists gnashed their teeth in rage at
their publication. The editor of the Collection, Kamenev, admitted to me openly with the not very modest
"kind-heartedness" that characterizes him: If the bloc
between us were not being prepared, he would never
under any circumstances have allowed the publication
of the document. In an article of Kostrcheva in
BOLSHEVIK, these theses are mendaciously falsified precisely for the purpose of not bringing Lenin under the
suspicion of the "Trotskyist" attitude towards the
peasantry as a whole and the middle peasants in particular.

I quote here further Lenin's evaluation of his differences of opinion with me, which he presented in
1909:

"Comrade Trotsky himself, in this instance, grants
'the participation of the representatives of the democratic population' in the 'workers' government', that
is, *he grants a government of representatives of the
proletariat and the peasantry.* Under what conditions
the participation of the proletariat in the government
of the revolution is permissible—remains a separate
question, and in this question, the Bolsheviks will most
likely not come to an agreement not only with Trotsky, but also with the Polish social democracy. The
question of the dictatorship of the revolutionary classes, however, is in no case reduced to the question of
the 'majority' in any revolutionary government, but
to the question of the conditions under which the par-

ticipation of the social democracy in any government
is permissible." (Volume XI, Part 1, page 229. My
emphasis. L. T.)

In this quotation from Lenin, it is again confirmed
that Trotsky accepts a government of representatives
of the proletariat and the peasantry, that is, does not
"skip over" the latter. Lenin emphasizes in this connection that the question of the dictatorship is not
reduced to the question of the majority in the government. This is incontestable. It is a question, in the
first place, of the common work of the proletariat and
peasantry and consequently of the struggle of the
proletarian vanguard against the liberal or "national"
bourgeoisie for the influence over the peasants. But
if the question of the revolutionary dictatorship of
the workers and peasants is also *not reduced* to the
question of the majority in the government, it nevertheless inevitably *leads*, upon the victory of the revolution, to this question as the decisive one. As we have
seen, Lenin (in any case) cautiously makes the reservation: Should the question arise about the participation of the party in a revolutionary government, then
we will probably have a different opinion from Trotsky
as well as from the Polish comrades over the *conditions* of this participation. It was a matter therefore
of *probable* differences of opinion, in so far as Lenin
considered theoretically permissible the participation
of the representatives of the proletariat as a minority in the democratic government. Events, however,
showed that we were not of different opinions. In
November 1917, a struggle raged in the summits of
the party around the question of the coalition government with the Social Revolutionists and the Mensheviks. Lenin was not opposed in principle to a
coalition on the basis of the Soviets, but he categori-

cally demanded a firm safeguarding of the Bolshevik
majority. I went along with him hand in hand.

* * *

Now let us see what Radek is actually aiming at
with the whole question of the democratic dictatorship
of the proletariat and the peasantry:

"Wherein", he asks, "did the old Bolshevik theory
of 1905 prove to be fundamentally correct? In the
fact that the joint action of the Petrograd workers
and peasants (the soldiers of the Petrograd garrison)
overthrew czarism [in 1917. L. T.]. The formula
of 1905 foresees in its fundamentals only the relationship of the classes, and not a concrete political insti-
tution."

Well, well, well! When I designate the old Leninist
formula as "algebraic", that is, permitting of various
concrete interpretations, it is in no case for the purpose of permitting it to be converted into an empty
commonplace, as Radek does unhesitatingly. "The
fundamental point was realized: the proletariat and
the peasantry jointly overthrew czarism." But this
"fundamental" was accomplished without exception in
every victorious or semi-victorious revolution. Czars,
feudal lords, and priests were always and everywhere
beaten with the fists of the proletarian, or the precur-
sors of the proletarian, the plebeian and peasant. That
is how it was already in the sixteenth century in Germany and even earlier. In China it was also workers
and peasants who beat the militarists. What has
this to do with the democratic dictatorship? It did
not exist in the old revolutions, nor in China. Why
not? On the backs of the workers and peasants, who
did the dirty work of the revolution, sat the bourgeoisie. Radek has "strayed" so far from political institutions that he has forgotten what is "most funda-

mental" in the revolution: who leads and who seizes power? A revolution, however, is a struggle for power. It is a political struggle which the classes conduct not with empty hands but with the aid of the "political institutions" (party, etc.).

"People who have not thought out to the end the complexity of the method of Marxism and Leninism", Radek thunders against us sinners, "understand it this way: the affair must absolutely end with a joint government of the workers and peasants, yes, a few even imagined that it absolutely had to be a coalition government of the workers' and peasants' parties."

What blockheads these "few" are! . . . And what does Radek himself imagine? That a victorious revolution must not lead to a new government, or that this new government must not reflect and insure a definite relationship of forces of the revolutionary classes? Radek has deepened the "sociological" in such a way that nothing has been left of it but a shell of words.

How impermissible it is to digress from the question of the political forms of the collaboration of the workers and peasants, will best be shown to us by the words of one of Radek's lectures in the Communist Academy in March 1927:

"A year ago, I wrote an article in PRAVDA on this [Canton] government which I named *peasants' and workers' government*. The comrades of the editorial board, however, assumed that it was an oversight on my part and corrected it: *workers' and peasants' government*. I did not protest against this and let it stand: workers' and peasants' government."

Thus, in 1927 (not in 1905) Radek was of the opinion that there could be a peasants' and workers' government in distinction to a workers' and peasants'

government.   The editor of PRAVDA did not grasp
this. I admit, neither do I. What a workers' and
peasants' government is, we know. But what is a
peasants' and workers' government, in distinction and
in contrast to a workers' and peasants' government?
Perhaps you will take the time to explain to us this
mysterious transposition of adjectives? Here we are
approaching the heart of the question. In 1926,
Radek believed the Canton government of Chiang Kai-
Shek to be a peasants' and workers' government, in
1927 he repeated it with determination. In reality,
however, it proved to be a *bourgeois* government, which
only exploited for itself the revolutionary struggle of
the workers and peasants, and then drowned them in
blood. How is this error to be explained? Did Radek
simply deceive himself? One can be deceived at a distance. But then one must say: I did not understand
it, did not scrutinize it, I made a mistake. But no,
we have here no error in fact out of the lack of information, but rather, as now appears clear, a deep mistake in principle. The peasants' and workers' government in contrast to the workers' and peasants' government—that is the Kuo Min Tang. It can mean
nothing else. When the peasantry does not follow the
proletariat, it follows the bourgeoisie. I believe the
question has been sufficiently clarified in my criticism
of the Stalinist idea of "temporarily constituted workers' and peasants' parties" (see *The Draft Program of
the Comintern, A Criticism of Fundamentals*). The
Canton "peasants' and workers' government" in distinction from a workers' and peasants' government is,
in the language of present-day Chinese politics, the
only conceivable expression of the "democratic dictatorship" in contrast to the proletarian dictatorship,
in other words, the embodiment of the Stalinist Kuo

Min Tang policy in contrast to the Bolshevik policy
which the Communist International calls "Trotskyist".

IV

What Did the Theory of the Permanent

Revolution Look Like in Practise?

*I*N CRITICIZING the theory, Radek supplements it, as we have seen, by the *"tactics flowing from it"*. This is a very important supplement.   The official criticism of "Trotskyism" prudently limited itself in this question to the theory.   For Radek, however, this does not suffice.   He is conducting a struggle against a definite (Bolshevik) tactical line in China.   He must discredit this line by the theory of the permanent revolution, and here it is necessary to show, or to act as though somebody has already showed, that in the past the false tactical line flowed from this theory. Here Radek is directly misleading his readers.   It is possible that he himself does not know the history of the revolution, in which he never took a direct part. But obviously he has also not made the slightest effort to investigate the question with documents at hand.   The most important of these are contained in the second volume of my *Collected Works*: an investigation is thus possible for anybody who can read.

Let us therefore reveal to Radek: in almost all the

stages of the first revolution there existed between
Lenin and me a complete agreement in the estimation
of the forces of the revolution and its actual tasks,
in spite of the fact that I spent the whole of 1905
illegally in Russia and 1906 in prison.   I am compelled
to confine myself here to a minimum number of proofs
and illustrations.

In an article written in February and printed in
March, that is, two or three months before the first
Bolshevik convention (which passed into history as the
third convention), I said:

"The bitterest struggle between the people and
the czar, which knows no other thought than victory;
the popular insurrection as the culminating point of
this struggle; the provisional government as the revolutionary culmination of the victory of the people
over the centuries-old foe; the disarming of the czarist reaction and the arming of the people by the provisional government; the convocation of the constituent assembly on the basis of general, equal, direct
and secret suffrage—these are the objectively prescribed stages of the revolution." (Volume II, Part 1,
page 232.)

It is enough to compare these words with the resolutions of the Bolshevik convention of May 1905 in
order to recognize in the posing of the fundamental
tactical problems my complete solidarity with the Bolsheviks.

Even more, in the spirit of this article, I formulated
in Petersburg, in agreement with Krassin, the theses
on the provisional government which appeared illegally at that time.   Krassin defended them at the Bolshevik convention.   Lenin consented to them in the
following form:

"By and large, I share the opinion of comrade

Krassin. It is natural that, as a writer, I took into
account the literary side of the question. *The importance of the aim of the struggle is very correctly presented by comrade Krassin and I am with him completely.* One cannot engage in struggle without reck-
oning on capturing the position for which one is
fighting. . . . " (Volume VI, page 180.)

The largest part of the extensive Krassin amendments, to which I refer the reader, was adopted in the
resolution of the convention. That these amendments
are derived from me, is proved by a note from Krassin
which I still possess. This whole party episode is
well known to Kamenev and others.

The problems of the peasantry, their attraction to
the workers' Soviets, the question of the cooperation
with the peasants' league, engaged the attention of
the Peterburg Soviet more and more every day. Perhaps Radek still knows that the direction of the Soviets devolved upon me. Here is one of the hundreds
of formulations written by me at that time on the
tactical tasks of the revolution:

"The proletariat creates city 'Soviets' which direct
the fighting actions of the urban masses, and puts
upon the order of the day the fighting alliance with
the army and the peasantry." (NATCHALO, No. 4, 17-
30, November 1905.)

It is wearisome and, I must admit, painful, to adduce quotations which are to prove that there was no
question with me of a "leap" out of autocracy to
socialism. But I am compelled to do it. I wrote the
following, for example, in February 1906 on the tasks
of the constituent assembly, in no case, however, coun-
terposing it at the very outset to the Soviets, as Radek, following Stalin, now hastens to do in regard
to China in order to wipe out the opportunist traces

of yesterday with an ultra-Leftist broom:

"The constituent assembly will be convoked by the liberated people by its own power. The tasks of the constituent assembly will be gigantic. It will have to reconstruct the state upon a democratic foundation, that is, upon the foundation of the sovereign people's power. It will establish a people's militia, carry out an enormous land reform, and introduce the eight-hour day and a progressive income tax." (Volume II, Part 1, page 349.)

And now, especially on the question of the "immediate" introduction of socialism, from the popular leaflet written by me in 1905:

"Is it possible to introduce socialism in Russia immediately? No, our village is still too dark and too unenlightened. There are too few real socialists among the peasants. First and foremost, the autocracy, which keeps the masses of the people in darkness, must be overthrown. The village poor must be freed of all taxation; the progressive income tax, universal compulsory education, must be introduced; finally, the land proletariat and semi-proletariat must be united with the city proletariat into a social democratic army. Only such an army will be in a position to carry through the great socialist revolution." (Volume II, Part 1, page 228.)

This almost sounds as though I did indeed differentiate between the democratic and socialist stages of the revolution, long before even Stalin and Thälmann, and now Radek too, began to teach me this.

Twenty-two years ago, I wrote:

"When the idea of the *uninterrupted* revolution was formulated in the socialist press, a revolution which— *through growing social clashes, uprisings of ever new sections of the people, incessant attacks of the pro-*

*letariat upon the political and economic privileges of
the ruling classes—combines the liquidation of absolutism and serfdom with the socialist revolution,* our
'progressive' press unanimously raised a furious howl."
(*Our Revolution,* 1906, page 258.)

First of all, I should like to call attention to the
definition of the uninterrupted revolution contained in
these words: it combines the liquidation of the Middle
Ages with the socialist revolution through a series of
growing social clashes. Where is the leap here? Where
is the ignoring of the democratic stage? And isn't
this what actually happened in 1917?

Let us establish in passing that the howling of the
"progressive" press of 1905 over the uninterrupted
revolution can stand no comparison with the in no way
progressive howling of the present-day writers who
have intervened in the affair after a brief delay of a
quarter of a century.

What was the attitude of the then leading organ of
the Bolshevik faction, Novaïa Zhizn, which appeared
under the vigilant editorship of Lenin, to the question
of the permanent revolution raised by me in the press?
Surely, the question is not devoid of interest. To the
article of the "radical" bourgeois journal, Nasha
Zhizn, which had endeavored to set up the "more
rational" views of Lenin against the "permanent revolution" of Trotsky, the Bolshevik Novaïa Zhizn replied (on November 27, 1905):

"This gratuitous report is of course sheer nonsense.
Comrade Trotky said that the proletarian revolution,
without standing still at the first stage, by pressing
hard upon the exploiters, can continue on its road,
while Lenin pointed out that the political revolution
is only the first step. The publicist of Nasha Zhizn
would like to perceive a contradiction there . . . The

whole misunderstanding comes, first, from the fear with
which the name alone of the social revolution fills
NASHA ZHIZN, secondly, out of the desire of this paper
to discover some sort of a sharp and piquant difference
of opinion among the social democrats, and thirdly,
in the metaphorical expression of comrade Trotsky:
'at one fell swoop'.   In No. 10 of NATCHALO, comrade
Trotsky explains his ideas quite unequivocally:

" 'The complete victory of the revolution signifies
the victory of the proletariat', writes comrade Trotsky. 'But this victory in turn signifies the further
uninterruptedness of the revolution.   The proletariat
realizes the fundamental tasks of democracy and the
logic of its immediate struggle for the safeguarding
of political domination causes purely socialist problems to arise at the given moment.   Between the minimum and the maximum program of the social democracy, a revolutionary continuity is established.   This
is not one "blow", it is not one day and not a month,
it is a whole historical epoch.   It would be absurd
to want to determine its duration in advance.' "

This reference alone exhausts, to a certain degree,
the theme of this brochure.   Could all the subsequent criticism of the epigones be pushed aside in advance more clearly, more precisely, more surely than
was done in those of my newspaper articles which
Lenin's NOVAÏA ZHIZN quoted so approvingly? My article set forth that the victorious proletariat, in the
process   of the realization of the democratic tasks,
would inevitably be confronted at a certain stage, by
the logic of its position, by purely socialist problems.
That is just where the *continuity* lies between the minimum and maximum programs, which grows inevitably
out of the dictatorship of the proletariat.   This is
not a blow, it is not a leap—I explained to my critics

in the camp of the petty bourgeoisie of that time—
it is a whole historical epoch. And Lenin's Novaïa
Zhizn associated itself completely with this perspective. Even more important, I hope, is the fact that
the actual course of development tested it and in 1917
finally confirmed it as correct.

Outside of the petty bourgeois democrats of Nasha
Zhizn, it was mainly the Mensheviks who, in 1905 and
particularly in 1906, after the defeat of the revolution
had begun, spoke of the fantastic "leap" over democracy to socialism. Among the Mensheviks, it was
especially Martinov and the deceased Jordansky who
distinguished themselves in this field. Both of them,
be it said in passing, later became stalwart Stalinists.
To the Menshevik writers who sought to hang the
"leap to socialism" on me, I expounded, in a special
article written in 1906, in detail and popularly, not
only the error but also the stupidity of such a contention, which I could reprint today, almost un-
abridged, against the criticism of the epigones. But
it will perhaps suffice to say that the résumé of the
article reached its culminating point in the following
words:

"I understand quite well—as I must needs assure
my reviewer [Jordansky]—that a publicistic leap over
a political obstacle is far from signifying its practical
surmounting." (Volume II, Part 1, page 454.)

Perhaps this will suffice? In case it does not—I
can continue so that my critics, like Radek, will not
be able to refer to the fact that they did not have "at
hand" that over which they pass judgment so cava-
lierly.

Our Tactic, the brochure written by me in prison
in 1906 and published immediately by Lenin, is characterized by the following conclusion:

"The proletariat will be able to support itself upon
the uprising of the village and, in the cities, the centers
of political life, it will be in a position to complete the
affair it was able to begin.   Supported by the peasant
element and leading it, the proletariat will not only
deal reaction the final triumphant blow, but it will
also understand how to secure the victory of the revolution."   (Volume II, Part 1, page 448.)

Does this look like an ignoring of the peasantry?

In   the   same   brochure,   moreover,   the following
thought also is developed:

"Our tactic, calculated upon the irresistible development of the revolution, must of course not ignore
the inevitable or the possible or even only the probable phases and stages of the revolutionary movement."   (Volume II, Part 1, page 436.)

Does this look like a fantastic leap?

In   the   article   *The Lessons of the First Soviets*
(1906), I depict the perspective of the further development of the revolution (or, as happened in reality,
of the new revolution) in the following manner:

"History does not repeat itself—and the new Soviet
will not have to go through once more the events of
the fifty days (October to December 1905); but for
that it will be able to borrow its program of action
completely from this period.   This program is completely clear.   Revolutionary cooperation with the
army, the peasantry, and the lowest strata of the city
petty bourgeoisie.   Abolition of absolutism.   Destruction of its material organization: partial rebuilding of
the formations, partial dissolution of the army, destruction of the bureaucratic police apparatus, eight-
hour day, arming of the population, above all of the
proletariat.   Transformation of the Soviets into organs of the revolutionary city self-administration.

creation of Soviets of peasants' deputies (peasant committees) on the land, as organs of the agrarian revolution, organization of the elections to the constituent assembly and electoral struggle on the basis of a definite labor program of the people's representatives." (Volume II, Part 2, page 206.)

Does this look like a skipping of the agrarian revolution, or an underestimation of the peasant question as a whole? Does this look as though I did not see the democratic tasks of the revolution? No, it does not. But what then does the political daubing of Radek look like? Nothing at all.

Graciously, but very ambiguously, Radek draws a line between my position of 1905, which he distorts, and the position of the Mensheviks, without it occurring to him that he is himself repeating three-fourths of the Menshevik criticism: Even though Trotsky employed the same method as the Mensheviks, Radek explains jesuitically, his aim was nevertheless different. By this subjective description, Radek completely discredits his own attitude on the question. Lassalle already knew that the aim depends upon the method and in the final analysis is conditioned by it. He even wrote a drama, as is known, on this theme *(Franz von Sickingen)*. But in what lay the similarity of my method with that of the Mensheviks? In the attitude towards the peasantry. As evidence, Radek adduces three polemical lines out of the 1916 article by Lenin which I have already quoted, observing himself, however, in passing that here Lenin, although he names Trotsky, was in reality polemicizing against Bucharin and against himself, that is, Radek. Besides this quotation from Lenin which, as we have already seen, is refuted by the whole content of Lenin's article, Radek makes reference to—Trotsky himself. Exposing the emptiness of the Menshevik conception, I asked in 1916 in an article: If it is not the liberal bourgeoisie that will lead, then who? You, Mensheviks, do not at any rate believe in the *independent* political rôle of the peasantry. The Mensheviks had the view that it is impermissible to "repulse" the liberal bourgeoisie for the sake of a dubious and unreliable alliance with the peasantry. This was the "method" of the Mensheviks. While mine consisted of pushing the liberal bourgeoisie aside and fighting for the leadership of the revolutionary peasantry. In this fundamental question I had no differences with Lenin. And when I said to the Mensheviks in the course of the struggle against them: "You least of all are prepared to assign a leading rôle to the peasantry", then this was no agreement with the method of the Mensheviks, as Radek seeks to insinuate, but rather a clear alternative: either the dictatorship of the liberal plutocracy or the dictatorship of the proletariat.

The same, completely correct argument that I made in 1916 against the Mensheviks, which Radek disloyally tries to utilize against me also, was used by me nine years before that, at the London congress of 1907, when I defended the theses of the Bolsheviks on the attitude towards the non-proletarian parties. I present here the fundamental part of my London speech which, in the first years of the revolution, was often reprinted in anthologies and textbooks as the expression of the Bolshevik attitude towards the classes and the parties in the revolution:

"To the comrades of the Menshevik ranks, their own views appear unusually complicated. I have repeatedly heard accusations from them that I over-simplified the description of the course of the Russian revolution. Despite the external amorphousness, which invests it

with that complex appearance—indeed just because
of this amorphousness—the views of the Mensheviks
may be reduced to a very simple schema which should
be accessible even to the understanding of Mr. Miliukov.

"In the postcript to the recently published book,
*How Did the Elections to the Second State Duma Turn
Out?* the ideological leader of the Cadet party writes:
'As to the Left groups in the narrower sense of the
word, that is, the socialist and revolutionary groups,
an agreement with them will be more difficult. But
even here, again, there are, if not decidedly positive,
then at least very weighty negative reasons which,
up to a certain point, can facilitate an approach.
Their aim is—to criticize and to discredit us; for that
alone it is necessary that we be present and act. As
we know, to the socialists, not only in Russia, but
throughout the world, the revolution now taking place
signifies—a bourgeois and not a socialist revolution:
a revolution which is to be accomplished by the bourgeois democracy. To capture the place of this democracy . . . for this the socialists of the whole world have
not prepared, and if the country has sent them into
the Duma in such great numbers, then it was certainly not for the purpose of realizing socialism now
or in order to carry through the necessary "bourgeois"
reforms with their own hands . . . It will consequently
be more profitable for them to criticize the rôle of
the parliamentarians rather than to compromise themselves in the same rôle.'

"As we see, Miliukov leads us to the very heart
of the question. The quotation cited gives all the
most important elements of the Menshevik attitude
towards the revolution and the relationship between
bourgeois and socialist democracy.

" 'The revolution that is taking place is a bour-geois and not a socialist revolution'—that's the first thing. The bourgeois revolution 'must be realized by the bourgeois democracy'—that's the second point. The socialist democracy cannot carry through bour-geois reforms with its own hands, its rôle is a purely oppositional one: 'Criticize and discredit'. And final-ly—as the fourth point—in order for the socialists to obtain the possibility of remaining in the opposi-tion, 'it is necessary that we [that is, the bourgeois democracy] be present and act'.

"And if 'we' are not present? And if there is no bourgeois democracy capable of marching at the head of the bourgeois revolution? Then it must be in-vented. This is just the conclusion to which Men-shevism arrives. It builds up the bourgeois democracy, and its attributes and history, out of its own imagina-tion.

"As materialists, we must in the first place pose the question of the social bases of the bourgeois democ-racy: upon what strata and classes can it support itself?

"It is needless to speak about the big bourgeoisie as a revolutionary power—on this we are all united. Lyons industrialists, even in the great French revo-lution, which was a national revolution in the broad-est sense of the term, played a counter-revolutionary rôle. But we are told about the middle bourgeoisie, and particularly of the petty bourgeoisie, as the leading force of the bourgeois revolution. But what does this petty bourgeoisie represent?

"The Jacobins supported themselves upon the city democracy, which grew up out of the guilds. Small masters, assistants, and the city population closely bound up with them, constituted the army of the rev-

olutionary *sansculottes*, the prop of the leading party
of the Montagnards. It was precisely this compact
mass of the city population, which had gone through
the long historical school of the guild, that bore upon
its shoulders the whole burden of the revolutionary
overturn. The objective result of the revolution was
the creation of 'normal' conditions of capitalist exploitation. The social mechanics of the historical
process, however, led to the point where the conditions
were created for the domination of the bourgeoisie
by the plebs, the democracy of the streets, the *sansculottes*. Their terrorist dictatorship purged bourgeois society of the old rubbish and then, after it had
overthrown the dictatorship of the petty bourgeois
democracy, the bourgeoisie came to rule.

"Now I ask over and over again: What social class
in our country will elevate revolutionary bourgeois democracy, put it in power, and give it the possibility of
carrying out the gigantic work, if the proletariat remains in opposition? I have again and again asked
the Mensheviks for a reply to this central question.
It is true, we have enormous masses of the revolutionary peasantry. But the comrades of the minority
know just as well as I do that the peasantry, regardless of how revolutionary it may be, is incapable of
playing an *independent*, much less a *leading*, political
rôle. The peasantry can undoubtedly prove to be
an enormous power in the service of the revolution;
but it would be unworthy of a Marxist to believe that
a peasant party is capable of placing itself at the
head of a bourgeois revolution and, upon its own initiative, liberate the productive forces of the country
from the archaic fetters. The city has the hegemony
in modern society and the hegemony in the bourgeois

revolution can belong to it alone*.

"Now where have we the city democracy that is capable of leading the people? Comrade Martinov has already sought it repeatedly, magnifying glass in hand. He found Saratov teachers, Petersburg lawyers, and Moscow statisticians. Like all his colleagues, he too would take no notice at all of the fact that in the Russian revolution the industrial proletariat will occupy the ground upon which the semi-proletarian artisan's democracy of the *sansculottes* stood at the end of the eighteenth century. I call your attention, comrades, to this fundamental principle fact.

"Our big industry did not develop naturally out of handicrafts. The economic history of our towns does not know the period of guilds. Capitalist industry with us arose under the direct and immediate pressure of European capital. It really conquered a virginal primitive soil, without encountering the resistance of handicraft culture. Foreign capital flowed into our country through the channels of state loans and through the pipes of private initiative. It gathered around itself the army of the industrial proletariat and prevented the rise and development of handicrafts. As a result of this process there appeared among us as the main power of the city, at the moment of the bourgeois revolution, an industrial proletariat of the highest social type. This is a fact that cannot be disputed and which must be taken as the basis of our revolutionary tactical conclusions.

"If the comrades of the minority [the Mensheviks] believe in the victory of the revolution, or even only

* Do the belated critics of the permanent revolution agree with this? Are they prepared to extend this principle also to the countries of the East, China, India, etc.? —Yes or no?

recognize the possibility of such a victory, they cannot dispute the fact that in our country there is no other historical claimant to revolutionary power than the proletariat. Just as the petty bourgeois city democracy in the great revolution placed itself at the head of the revolutionary nation, so the proletariat, the only revolutionary democracy of our cities, must find a support in the peasant masses and place itself in power—if the revolution has any prospect of victory at all.

"*A government supported directly upon the proletariat, and through it upon the revolutionary peasantry, does not yet signify the socialist dictatorship.* I do not touch upon the further perspectives of a proletarian government now. Perhaps the proletariat is condemned to collapse, as the Jacobin democracy collapsed in order to give way to the rule of the bourgeoisie. I want to establish only one point: If the revolutionary movement in our country, as Plechanov foretold, triumphs as a workers' movement, then the victory of the revolution is possible only as the revolutionary victory of the proletariat—otherwise it is altogether impossible.

"I insist upon this conclusion with all determination. If it is assumed that the social antagonisms between the proletariat and the peasant masses will prevent the proletariat from placing itself at the head of the movement; that, further, the proletariat is not strong enough for a victory—then one must arrive at the conclusion that no victory is destined for our revolution. Under such circumstances, an agreement between the liberal bourgeoisie and the old power would have to be the natural *finale* of the revolution. This is a conclusion, the possibility of which can in no case be contested. But it is clear that it is based upon the line of the defeat of the revolution, conditioned by its internal weakness. *The entire analysis of the Mensheviks—above all their evaluation of the proletariat and its possible relationship to the peasantry— leads them inexorably to the path of revolutionary pessimism.*

"But they persistently deviate from this path and develop a revolutionary optimism on the credit . . . of the bourgeois democracy.

"Thence results its relationship to the Cadets. The Cadets are for them the symbol of bourgeois democracy, and bourgeois democracy—the natural claimant to revolutionary power. . . .

.   .   .   .

"Upon what do you base your belief that the Cadet will still rise and stand erect?   Upon facts of political development?   No, upon your schema.   In order 'to carry the revolution through to the end' you need the city bourgeois democracy, you search after it eagerly, and find nothing but Cadets.   And you develop at their expense a rare optimism, you dress them up, you force them to play a creative rôle, a rôle which they do not want to play, cannot play and will not play. To my central question—I have put it repeatedly—I have heard no response. You have no prognosis of the revolution. Your policy is destitute of any great perspectives whatsoever.

"And in connection with this, your relationship to the bourgeois parties is formulated in words which the convention should bear firmly in mind: 'as the occasion requires'.   The proletariat does not carry on the systematic struggle for influence over the masses of the people, it does not check up its tactical steps from the angle of the single leading thought: to gather around it the weary and the heavy-laden and to be-

come their herald and leader." (*Minutes and Resolutions of the Fifth Convention*, pages 180-185.)

This speech, which sums up briefly all my articles,
speeches and acts of 1905 and 1906, was completely
approved by the Bolsheviks, not to speak of Rosa
Luxemburg and Tyschko (on the basis of this speech,
we entered upon more intimate relations which led
to my collaboration in their Polish journal). Lenin,
who could not forgive me my conciliatory conduct
toward the Mensheviks—and he was right—expressed
himself on my speech with a deliberately underlined
reserve. He said:

"I merely wish to observe that Trotsky, in his book
On the Defense of the Party emphatically expressed
his solidarity with Kautsky, who wrote of the economic
community of interests of the proletariat and the
peasantry in the present revolution in Russia. Trotsky recognized the admissibility and expediency of a
Left bloc [with the peasants. L. T.] against the liberal bourgeoisie. These facts are enough for me to
establish Trotsky's approach to our conception. *Independent of the question of the 'uninterrupted revolution'*, we have here before our eyes a solidarity in
the fundamental points of the question concerning the
relationship to the bourgeois parties." (Lenin, Volume VIII, page 400.)

Lenin occupied himself in his speech all the less with
a rounded evaluation of the theory of the permanent
revolution since I too, in my speech, had not developed the further perspectives of the dictatorship of
the proletariat. He had obviously not read my fundamental work on this question, otherwise he would not
have spoken of my "approach" to the conception of
the Bolsheviks as of something new, for my London
speech was only a condensed reproduction of my

works of 1905-1906. He expressed himself very re-
servedly, because I did stand outside the Bolshevik faction. In spite of that, or more correctly, perhaps precisely because of that, his words allow no room for
false interpretations. Lenin established the "solidarity in the fundamental points of the question" of
the relationship to the peasantry and to the liberal
bourgeoisie. This solidarity does not relate to my
aims, as Radek preposterously represents it, but precisely to the *method*. As to the perspectives of the
democratic revolution growing into the socialist revolution, it is right here that Lenin makes the reservation, "independent of the question of the uninterrupted revolution". What is the meaning of this
reservation? It is clear that Lenin in no way identified the permanent revolution with the ignoring of the
peasantry or with skipping over the agrarian revolution, as has been done by the ignorant and unscrupu-
lous epigones, who have made a rule of it. This is
Lenin's idea: How far our revolution will go, whether
the proletariat can come to power in our country
sooner than in Europe and what perspectives this
opens up for socialism—these questions I do not touch
upon; however, in the fundamental question of the relationship of the proletariat to the peasantry and to
the liberal bourgeoisie the *"solidarity is before our
eyes"*.

We have seen above the echo which the theory of
the permanent revolution produced almost immediately
after its origination, that is, already in 1905, in the
Bolshevik NOVAÏA ZHIZN. We want to refer further
to how the editors of Lenin's *Collected Works* expressed themselves on this theory after 1917. In the annotations to Volume XIV, Part 2. page 481, it says:

"Already before the 1905 revolution he [Trotsky]

advanced the original and *now especially noteworthy*
theory of the permanent revolution, in which he con-
tended that *the bourgeois revolution of 1905 would
pass directly over into a socialist revolution,* and then
constitute the first of a series of national revolutions."

I admit that this is no acknowledgment of the correctness of all that I have written on the permanent
revolution.   But in any case it is an acknowledgment
of the incorrectness of what Radek writes about it.
"The *bourgeois* revolution will pass directly over into
a socialist revolution"—but this is precisely the theory
of the *growing into* and not of *skipping over;* from
that comes a realistic, and not an adventuristic, tactic.   And what is the meaning of the words: "*now
especially noteworthy* theory of the permanent revolution"?   They mean that the October overthrow showed in a new light those sides of the theory which had
formerly remained in obscurity for many or had simply appeared "improbable".   The second part of Volume XIV of Lenin's *Collected Works* appeared while
their author was alive.   Thousands upon thousands of
party members read this annotation.   And nobody declared it to be false until the year 1924.   It occurred
to Radek, however, to do this—in the year 1928.

But in so far as Radek speaks not only of the theory
but also of the tactic, the most important argument
against him still remains the character of my practical
participation in the revolutions of 1905 and 1917.
My work in the Petersburg Soviet of 1905 coincided
with the elaboration of those of my views on the nature
of the revolution which the epigones now expose to an
uninterrupted fire.   How could such allegedly erroneous views fail to be reflected in my political activity,
which was carried on before the eyes of the whole world
and registered every day in the press?   But if it is

assumed that such an absurd theory was expressed in
my policy, then why did the present Consuls remain
silent at that time? And what is to a certain extent
even more important, why did Lenin at that time most
energetically defend the line of the Petrograd Soviets,
at the high point of the revolution as well as after its
defeat?

The same questions, only perhaps more sharply
formulated, relate to the revolution of 1917. In New
York, I wrote a series of articles on the February revolution from the point of view of the theory of the
permanent revolution. All these articles are today
reprinted. My tactical conclusions coincided entirely
with the conclusions which Lenin drew at the same
time in Geneva, and consequently, were in the same
irreconcilable contradiction to the conclusions of Kamenev, Stalin and the other epigones. When I arrived
in Petrograd, nobody asked me if I renounced my "errors" of the permanent revolution. Nor was there
anybody to ask. Stalin slunk around in embarrass-
ment from one corner to another and had only the one
desire that the party should forget as quickly as possible the policy which he had advocated up to Lenin's
arrival. Yaroslavksy was not yet the chairman of the
Control Commission: together with the Mensheviks,
with Ordjonikidze and others, he was publishing a
banal semi-liberal sheet in Yakutsk. Kamenev accused
Lenin of Trotskyism and declared when he met me:
"Now the celebration is on your street." On the eve
of the October, I wrote in the central organ of the
Bolsheviks on the perspectives of the permanent revolution. It never occurred to anybody to come out
against me. My solidarity with Lenin turned out to
be a complete and unconditional one. What can my
critics, among them Radek too, say now? That I my-

self had completely misunderstood the theory which I advocated, and that in the responsible historical periods, contrary to this theory, I acted entirely right? Is it not simpler to assume that my critics did not understand the permanent revolution, like so many other things? For if it is assumed that these tardy critics are well acquainted not only with their own ideas, but with those of others, then how is it to be explained that all of them, without exception, adopted such a miserable position in the revolution of 1917 and forever covered themselves with shame in the Chinese revolution?

*   *   *

But after all, many readers will suddenly recall, What about your most important tactical slogan: "Without the czar, but a labor government"?

This serves as a decisive argument in certain articles. Trotsky's frightful slogan: "Without the czar!" runs through all the writings of the various critics of the permanent revolution; with some it emerges as the final, most important and decisive argument; with others, as the ready harbor of weary thought.

This criticism naturally reaches its greatest profundity in the "Master"* of ignorance and disloyalty, when he says in his incomparable *Problems of Leninism*:

"We do not want to expatiate further [now then! L. T.] on the position of comrade Trotsky in 1905, where he 'simply' forgot the peasantry as a revolutionary force and raised the slogan: 'Without the czar —but a labor government', that is, the slogan for a revolution without the peasantry." (Stalin, *Problems*

* In a speech, Stalin once called himself the "Master of the revolution".

of Leninism, pages 174-175.)

Despite my positively hopeless position before this annihilating criticism, which does not want to "expatiate", I should nevertheless like to refer to some mitigating circumstances. There are some. I beseech a hearing.

Even if, in 1905, I had formulated an ambiguous or unhappy slogan in some article or other, which was open to misunderstanding, then today, twenty-three years later, it should not be considered in an isolated manner, but in connection with my other works on this theme, mainly, however, in connection with my political participation in the events. It simply does not do for me to call the reader's attention to the bare name of a work unknown to him (in the same way as to the critics) and to attribute a meaning to this name which stands in complete contradiction to everything I wrote and did.

Perhaps, too, it is not superfluous to add—O my critics!—that the slogan: "Without the czar—but a labor government" was never written, nor expressed, nor proposed by me! At the basis of the main argument of my judges there lies, aside from everything else, a shameful factual error. The fact of the matter is that a proclamation entitled "Without the czar —but a labor government" was written and published abroad in 1905 by Parvus. I had been living illegally for a long time in Petersburg in those days, and had no connections at all with this leaflet either in ideas or in fact. I learned of it much later from polemical articles. I never had the occasion or opportunity to express myself on it. As for the proclamation I (as, moreover, all my critics) neither saw it nor read it. This is the factual side of this fanciful affair. I am sorry that I must deprive all the

Thälmanns and Semards of this easily transportable
and convincing argument. But facts are stronger
than my humane feelings.

Still more. The incident providently added one
thing to the other: at the same time that Parvus published abroad the proclamation unknown to me "*Without the czar—but a labor government*", a leaflet
written by me appeared illegally in Petersburg with
the title: "*Neither czar nor Zemtsi,** but the people*".
This title, which is frequently repeated in the text of
the leaflet as a slogan embracing the workers and the
peasants, is, so to speak, invented in order to refute in
a popular form the later contentions about skipping
the democratic stage of the revolution. The appeal
is reprinted in my *Works* (Volume II, Part 1, page
256). There also are my proclamations, published by
the Bolshevik Central Committee, to that peasantry
which, in the ingenious expression of Stalin, I "simply
forgot".

But even this is not yet all. Only a short time
ago, the meritorious Rafes, a theoretician and leader
of the Chinese revolution, wrote in the theoretical organ of the Central Committee of the Communist Party
of the Soviet Union of the same frightful slogan which
Trotsky raised in the *year 1917*. Not 1905, but 1917!
For the Menshevik Rafes, at any rate, there is some
excuse: almost up till 1920 he was a "minister" of
Petlura, and how could he, weighed down by the cares
of state of the struggle against the Bolsheviks, pay
any heed there to what was going on in the camp of
the October revolution? Well, and the editorial board

---

* The local autonomous administration, the "zemstvo", consisted of representatives of the landowners among the nobil-
ity ["zemtsi"].

of the organ of the Central Committee?   What of it!
—one idiocy more or less. . . .

"But how is that possible?" a conscientious reader
raised on the trash of recent years might call out.
"Weren't we taught in hundreds and thousands of
books and articles . . ."

"Yes, friends, taught; and that is just why we will
have to learn anew. These are the losses incurred
through the period of reaction. Nothing can be done
about it. History does not proceed in a straight line.
It has temporarily run into the blind alleys of Stalin."

V

Was the "Democratic Dictatorship" Realized by Us? And When?

*A*PPEALING TO Lenin, Radek contends that the democratic dictatorship was realized in the dual power of the Kerensky period. Yes, *many times,* and conditionally, Lenin put the question this way— that I admit. "Many times?" Radek becomes indignant and accuses me of assailing the most fundamental ideas of Lenin. But Radek is angry only because he is wrong. In *The Lessons of October,* which Radek like-wise submits to criticism after a protracted delay of about four years, I interpreted Lenin's words on the "realization" of the democratic dictatorship in the following manner:

"The democratic workers' and peasants' coalition could make its appearance only as an immature prod-uct, which did not attain real power—only as a ten-dency, but not as a fact." (Volume III, Part 1, page xxi.)

With regard to this interpretation, Radek writes: "This reproduction of one of the most outstanding theoretical chapters in the work of Lenin *is worth*

absolutely nothing." These words are followed by a
pathetic appeal to the traditions of Bolshevism, and
finally, the conclusion: "These questions are too important to be able to reply to them with a reference
to what Lenin *many times* said."

By this, Radek wants to evoke the image of my care-
less conduct against "one of the most outstanding" of
Lenin's ideas. But Radek is wasting indignation and
pathos for nothing. A bit of understanding would
be more in place here. My presentation, even though
very condensed, in *The Lessons of October*, does not
rest upon a sudden inspiration on the basis of quotations taken at second hand, but upon a genuine
thorough study of Lenin's writings. It reproduces
the essence of the Leninist idea on this question, while
the verbose presentation of Radek, despite the super-
fluity of quotations, does not leave behind it a single
living passage of Lenin's thoughts.

Why did I make use of the restrictive words "many
times"? Because that is how it really stood. Refer-
ences to the fact that the democratic dictatorship was
"realized in the dual power" ("in certain forms and
up to a certain point"), were made by Lenin only in
the period between April and October 1917, that is, *before the genuine realization of the democratic revolution had been completed.* Radek neither noticed, grasped, nor understood how to evaluate this. In the struggle against the present epigones, Lenin spoke extremely conditionally of the "realization" of the democratic
dictatorship, not as of a historical characteristic of
the period of the dual power—in this form it would
be plain nonsense—but by this he argued against those
who expected a second, improved edition of the independent democratic dictatorship. Lenin's words only
meant that there is not and will not be any democratic

dictatorship outside of the miserable miscarriage of the dual power, and that new weapons therefore had to be provided, that is, the slogan had to be changed. To contend that the coalition of the Mensheviks and the Social Revolutionists with the bourgeoisie, which refused the peasants the land and hounded the Bolsheviks—constituted the "realization" of the Bolshevik slogan, either means deliberately to pass off black as white or else to have lost one's head entirely.

With regard to the Mensheviks, an argument could be presented which would be analogous to a certain point to Lenin's argument against Kamenev: "You are waiting for the bourgeoisie to fulfill a 'progressive' mission in the revolution? This mission has already been realized: the political rôle of the Rodziankos, the Gutchkovs and Miliukovs is the maximum that the bourgeoisie is able to give, just as the Kerenskiad is the maximum of democratic revolution that could be realized as an independent stage."

Unmistakable anatomical features — rudiments — show that our ancestors had a tail. These features suffice to confirm the genetic unity of animate being. But to put it quite candidly, man has no tail. Lenin demonstrated to Kamenev the rudiments of the democratic dictatorship in the régime of the dual power, warning him that no new organ should be hoped for out of these rudiments. And we did not have an independent democratic dictatorship, even though we completed the democratic revolution more deeply, more resolutely, more purely than had ever been done anywhere else.

Radek should reflect upon the fact that if, in February to April, the democratic dictatorship had *actually* been realized, even Molotov would have recognized it. The party and the class understood the democratic dictatorship as a régime which mercilessly destroys the old state apparatus of the monarchy and completely liquidates manorial landed property. But there was not a trace of this in the Kerensky period. For the Bolshevik party, however, it was a question of the *actual realization of the revolutionary tasks*, and not in the revelation of certain sociological and historical "rudiments". Lenin, in order to enlighten his adversaries theoretically — demonstrated splendidly this symptom which had not attained any development. But still, nothing more than that. Radek, however, endeavors in all seriousness to convince us that in the period of the dual power, that is, of powerlessness, the "dictatorship" did exist and the democratic revolution was realized. Only, it was allegedly such a "democratic revolution", that Lenin's genius was required to recognize it. But this is just the thing that signifies that it was not realized. The real democratic revolution, namely, is a thing that every illiterate peasant in Russia or in China easily recognizes. The morphological features are surely in a worse plight. Despite the Russian lesson to Kamenev, there has been no success, for example, in having Radek finally perceive that in China, the democratic dictatorship (through the Kuo Min Tang), in Lenin's sense, was likewise "realized" more thoroughly and more completely than with us in the dual power, and that only hopeless simpletons can wait for an improved edition of "democracy" in China.

If the democratic dictatorship had only been realized with us in the form of the Kerenskiad, which played the rôle of an errand-boy to Lloyd George and Clemenceau, then we would have to say that history indulged in cruel mockery with the strategic slogans of the Bolsheviks. Fortunately, it is not so. The

Bolshevik slogan was realized in fact—not as a morphological illusion but as the greatest historical reality.   Only, it was realized *not before the October but
after the October*.   The peasant war, in the words of
Marx, supported the dictatorship of the proletariat.
The collaboration of the two classes was realized
through the October on a gigantic scale.   Now every
ignorant peasant grasped and felt, even without
Lenin's commentaries, that the Bolshevik slogan had
been carried through in life.   And Lenin himself esti-
mated the October revolution—its first stage—as the
true realization of the democratic revolution, and by
that also as the true, even if changed, realization of
the strategic slogan of the Bolsheviks.   The *whole*
Lenin must be considered.   And before all, the Lenin
after the October, when he surveyed and evaluated
events from a loftier watch-tower. Finally, Lenin must
be considered in the Leninist way, and not in that of
the epigones.

The question of the class character of the revolution and its "growing into" is submitted by Lenin
(after the October) to an analysis in his book against
Kautsky.   Here is a passage over which Radek should
reflect a bit.

"Yes, our revolution [the October revolution. L. T.]
is a bourgeois revolution so long as we march together
with the peasantry as a whole.   We were more than
clearly conscious of this, and said hundreds and thousands of times since 1905 that this necessary stage
of the historical process cannot be skipped over or
abolished by decree."

And further on:

"It happened just as we had foretold.   The course
of the revolution confirmed the correctness of our consideration.   At the beginning, together with the

'whole' peasantry against the monarchy, against the landowners, against the Middle Ages (and to that extent it remains a bourgeois, a bourgeois-democratic revolution). And then, together with the poorest peasantry, with the semi-proletarian, with all the exploited against capitalism, including the rich and the speculators of the village, and to that extent the revolution becomes a socialist revolution." (Volume XV, page 508.)

That is how Lenin spoke, not "many times" but always, or, more correctly, giving the course of the revolution, including the October, a conclusive, a generalizing, thorough appreciation—forever. "It happened just as we had foretold." The bourgeois democratic revolution was realized as a coalition of the workers and peasants. In the Kerenskiad? No, *in the first period after the October.* Is that right? It is. But, as we now know, it was not realized in the form of the democratic dictatorship, but in the form of the dictatorship of the proletariat. With that there also disappeared the necessity for the old algebraic formula.

If the conditional argument of Lenin against Kamenev in 1917 and the rounded-out Leninist characterization of the October revolution in the subsequent years are uncritically juxtaposed, then it follows that two democratic revolutions were "realized" in Russia. This is too much, all the more since the second is separated from the first by an armed uprising of the proletariat.

Now contrast the quotation just made from Lenin's book, *Kautsky the Renegade*, with the passage from my *Results and Perspectives* where, in the chapter on *The Proletarian Régime*, the first stage of the dictatorship and the perspective of its further development is outlined:

"The abolition of class serfdom will find the support of the *whole* peasantry, as a subjugated estate. The progressive income tax will find the support of the immense majority of the peasantry. But legislative measures for the protection of the land proletariat will not only find no active sympathy among the majority, but they will clash with the active resistance of a minority.

"The proletariat will be compelled to carry the class struggle into the village, and in this way violate that community of interests which indubitably exists among the peasantry as a whole, even if within relatively narrow boundaries. In the earliest moments of its domination, the proletariat will have to seek a support in the conflict of interests of the village poor and the village rich—of the land proletariat and the agricultural bourgeoisie." (*Our Revolution*, 1906, page 255.)

How all this resembles an "ignoring" of the peasantry and the complete "antagonism" of the two lines, Lenin's and mine!

The quotation from Lenin adduced above does not stand alone in his works. On the contrary, as is always the case with Lenin, the new formula, which events illuminate more penetratingly, becomes for him the axis of his speeches and his articles for a whole period of time. In March 1919, Lenin said:

"In October 1917, we seized power together with the peasantry as a whole. That was a bourgeois revolution, to the extent that the class struggle in the village had not yet developed." (Volume XVI, page 143.)

The following was said by Lenin at the party convention in March 1919:

"In a country where the proletariat was compelled

to take power with the aid of the peasantry, and where
the rôle of agent of the petty bourgeois revolution fell
to the proletariat—our revolution, up to the formation of the Committees of the Poor, that is, up to the
summer and even the fall of 1918, was in large measure
a bourgeois revolution." (Volume XVI, page 105.)

These words were frequently repeated by Lenin in
different variations and on divers occasions. Radek,
however, simply avoids this capital thought which decides the disputed question.

The proletariat took power together with the peasantry in October, says Lenin. By that alone, the
revolution was a bourgeois revolution. Is that right?
In a certain sense, yes. But this means that the *true*
democratic dictatorship of the proletariat and the
peasantry, that is, the one which actually destroyed
the régime of autocracy and serfdom, and snatched
the land from the feudalists, was accomplished not
before the October but only *after* the October; accomplished, to put it as Marx did, as the *dictatorship*
of the proletariat supported by the peasant war, to
begin only a few months later with the growing into
a socialist dictatorship. Is *this* incomprehensible?
Can differences of opinion prevail on this point *today?*

According to Radek, the "permanent" theory sins
by mixing up the bourgeois stage with the socialist.
In reality, however, the class dynamics so thoroughly
"mixed up", that is, *united* these two stages—that our
unfortunate metaphysician is no longer in a position
to keep the ends asunder.

Certainly, many gaps and many incorrect contentions can be found in *Results and Perspectives.* But
this work was written not in 1928, but considerably
before the October . . . before the 1905 October. The
question of the gaps in the theory of the permanent

revolution, or more correctly, in my motivations of
this theory at that time, is not even touched upon by
Radek, for, following his teachers—the epigones—he
attacks not the gaps but the strong sides of the theory,
those which the course of historical development confirmed, attacks them in the name of the essentially
false conclusions which he traces from Lenin's attitude
—not thoroughly studied and not thought out to the
very end by Radek.

The juggling with obsolete quotations is practised
in general by the whole school of epigones entirely
upon a specific plane, which nowhere intersects the
real historical process. But when the opponents of
"Trotskyism" have to occupy themselves with the
analysis of the real development of the October revolution, and occupy themselves with it seriously and
consistently—which happens to many of them from
time to time—then they inevitably arrive at formulations in the spirit of the theory which they reject. We
find the crassest proof of this in the works of A. Yakovlev, which are devoted to the history of the October
revolution. The class relationships of old Russia are
formulated by this author, today a prop of the ruling
faction* and undoubtedly more educated than the
other Stalinists, and particularly than Stalin himself,
as follows:

". . . We see a twofold limitedness of the peasants' uprising (March to October 1917). Raising
itself to the level of a peasant war, the uprising did not
overcome its limitedness, did not burst asunder the
confines of its immediate task: to destroy the neighboring landowner; did not transform itself into an organ-

* Yakovlev was recently appointed People's Commissar of
Agriculture of the U. S. S. R.

ized revolutionary movement; did not surmount the
character of an elementary rebellion that distinguishes
the peasant movement.

"The peasant uprising taken by itself—an elementary act, limited in its aim to the extermination of the
neighboring landowner—could not triumph, could not.
destroy the state power hostile to the peasantry, which
supported the landowner.   That is why the agrarian
movement was capable of winning only because it was
led by the corresponding city class . . . This is the
reason why the fate of the agrarian revolution, in the
final analysis, was decided not in the tens of thousands
of villages, but in the hundreds of cities.   Only the
working class, which was dealing the bourgeoisie a
mortal blow in the centers of the country, could turn
the peasant uprising into victory; only the victory of
the working class in the city could tear the peasant
movement out of the confines of an elemental clash of
a few tens of millions of peasants with a few tens of
thousands of landowners; only the victory of the working class, finally, could lay the foundation stone of
a new type of peasant organization, which united the
poor and middle peasantry not with the bourgeoisie but
with the working class.   The problem of the victory
of the peasant uprising was a problem of the victory
of the working class in the city.

"When the workers dealt the government of the
bourgeoisie a decisive blow in October, by the same
token they simultaneously solved the problem of the
victory of the peasant uprising."

And further on:

" . . . that is just why it happened that, by virtue of the historically given conditions in 1917, bourgeois Russia came forward in alliance with the landowners.   Even the most Left factions of the bourge-

oisie, like the Mensheviks and the Social Revolutionists, did not go beyond the conclusion of an agreement
favorable to the landowners. Therein lies the most
important difference between the conditions of the Russian revolution and the French revolution which took
place more than a hundred years ago . . . The peasant revolution could not triumph as a bourgeois revolution in 1917 [now then! L. T.]. Two roads were
open to it. *Either defeat under the blows of the united
forces of the bourgeoisie and the landowners or—
victory, as a movement that marches together with the
proletarian revolution and assists it to triumph. By
taking over the mission of the bourgeoisie in the great
French revolution, by taking over the task of leading
the agrarian democratic revolution, the working class
of Russia obtained the possibility of a victorious proletarian revolution.*" (*The Peasant Movement in 1917*,
State Publishing House, 1927, pages x-xi, xi-xii.)

What are the fundamental elements of Yakovlev's
arguments? The incapacity of the peasantry to play
an *independent* political rôle; the resultant inevitability of the hegemony of the city class; the inadequacy
of the Russian bourgeoisie for the rôle of leader in
the agrarian revolution; the resultant inevitability of
the leading rôle of the proletariat; its seizure of power
as leader of the agrarian revolution; finally, the dictatorship of the proletariat which supports itself upon
the peasant war and opens up an epoch of socialist
revolutions. This destroys to the roots the metaphysical posing of the question concerning the "bourgeois"
or the "socialist" character of the revolution. The
kernel of the matter lay in the fact that the agrarian
question, which constituted the basis of the bourgeois
revolution, could not be solved under the rule of the
bourgeoisie. The dictatorship of the proletariat ap-

peared on the scene not *after* the completion of the agrarian democratic revolution but as the necessary *prerequisite* for its accomplishment. In a word, in this retrospective schema of Yakovlev, we have all the fundamental elements of the theory of the permanent revolution as formulated by me in 1905. With me, it was a question of a historical prognosis; Yakovlev, relying upon the preliminary studies of a whole staff of young research workers, draws conclusions from the lessons of the three revolutions twenty-two years after the first revolution and ten years after the October revolution. And then? Yakovlev repeats almost literally my formulation of 1905.

What is Yakovlev's attitude, however, to the theory of the permanent revolution? Such as befits a Stalinist official who wants to retain his post and even to climb to a higher one. But how does Yakovlev, in this case, reconcile his analysis of the driving forces of the October revolution with the struggle against "Trotskyism"? Very simply: he does not give a thought to such a reconciliation. Like many liberal czarist officials, who acknowledged Darwin's theory, but at the same time appeared punctually at communion, Yakovlev too pays for the right to express Marxian ideas from time to time with the price of participating in the ritual of baiting the permanent revolution. Such examples could be instanced by the dozen.

There still remains to add that Yakovlev did not execute the above-quoted work on the history of the October revolution on his own initiative, but on the basis of a decision of the Central Committee, which at the same time charged me with the editing of Yakovlev's work*. At that time, Lenin's recovery was

* Excerpt from the minutes of the session of the Organiza-

still expected, and it never occurred to any of the epigones to kindle an artificial dispute around the theory of the permanent revolution. At any rate, as the former, or more correctly, as the contemplated editor of the official history of the October revolution, I can establish with complete satisfaction that the author, in all the disputed questions, consciously or unconsciously employed the literal formulations of my persecuted and heretical work on the theory of the permanent revolution (*Results and Perspectives*).

The rounded-out evaluation of the historical fate of the Bolshevik slogan which Lenin himself gave, shows with certainty that the difference of the two lines, the "permanent" and Lenin's had an incidental and subordinated significance; what united them, however, was the principle. And this principle of both lines, which were completly fused by the October, is in irreconcilable antagonism not only to the February-March line of Stalin and the April-October line of Kamenev, Rykov and Zinoviev, not only to the whole China policy of Stalin, Bucharin and Martinov, but also to the present "Chinese" line of Radek.

And when Radek, who changed his judgment of values so radically between 1925 and the second half of 1928, seeks to convict me of not understanding "the complexity of Marxism and Leninism", then I can reply: The *fundamental* train of thought which I developed twenty-five years ago in *Results and Perspectives*, I consider confirmed by events as completely correct, and precisely because of that in agreement with the strategical line of Bolshevism.

tion Bureau of the Central Committee of May 22, 1922, under No. 21: "To commission comrade Yakovlev . . . to compile a textbook on the history of the October revolution under the editorial supervision of comrade Trotsky."

Especially do I fail to see the slightest cause to withdraw anything from what I said in 1922 on the permanent revolution in the foreword to my book *1905*, which the whole party read and studied in innumerable editions and reprints while Lenin was alive, and which "disturbed" Kamenev only in the autumn of 1924 and Radek, for the first time, in the autumn of 1928.

"Right in the period between January 9 and the October 1905 strike [it says in the foreword] the author formed those opinions on the character of the revolutionary development of Russia which later received the name 'theory of the permanent revolution'. This somewhat unusual name expressed the idea that the Russian revolution, standing before directly bourgeois aims, could in no case remain standing there. *The revoluton will not be able to solve its immediate bourgeois tasks except by putting the proletariat in power. . . .*

"This view, even if after a lapse of twelve years, was confirmed as completely correct. The Russian revolution could not terminate with the bourgeois democratic régime. It had to transfer power to the working class. *If the working class was still too weak for the capture of power in 1905, it had to mature and grow strong not in the bourgeois democratic republic but in the illegality of the* 'Third of June czarism*.' " (L. Trotsky, *1905*, foreword, page 45.)

I want to quote one more of the sharpest polemical judgments which I passed over the slogan of the 'democratic dictatorship". In 1909, I wrote in the

---

* On June 3 [16], 1907, the coup d'état was completed which formally inaugurated the period of triumphant counter-revolution.

Polish organ of Rosa Luxemburg:

"If the Mensheviks, proceeding from the abstraction that 'our revolution is bourgeois', arrive at the idea of adapting the whole tactic of the proletariat to the conduct of the liberal bourgeoisie, inclusive of their capture of state power, the Bolsheviks. proceeding from the same naked abstraction: 'democratic, not socialist dictatorship', arrive at the idea of the bourgeois democratic self-limitation of the proletariat in whose hands lies the state power. The difference between them in this question is certainly quite important: while the anti-revolutionary sides of Menshevism are already expressed in full force today, the anti-revolutionary features of Bolshevism threaten to be a great danger only in the event of the revolutionary victory."

To this passage in the article, which is reprinted in the Russian edition of my book *1905*, I made the following annotation:

"As is known, this did not take place, for Bolshevism, under the leadership of Lenin (though not without internal struggle), accomplished its ideological re-armament in this most important question in the spring of 1917, that is, before the seizure of power."

These two quotations have been subjected since 1924 to an onslaught of criticism. Now, after a delay of four years, Radek has also joined in with this criticism. Yet, if one reflects conscientiously upon the quoted lines, it must be admitted that they contained an important prognosis and a no less important warning. The fact does remain that at the moment of the February revolution the whole socalled "old guard" of the Bolsheviks stood on the ground of the stark contrasting of the democratic and socialist dictatorships. Out of Lenin's "algebraic" formula (allowing of many "arithmetical" interpretations), his closest disciples made a purely metaphysical construction and directed it against the real development of the revolution. At the most important historical turning point, the leadership of the Bolsheviks in Russia adopted a reactionary position, and had Lenin not arrived so opportunely, they would have been in a position to strangle the October revolution in the name of the struggle against Trotskyism, as they later strangled the Chinese revolution. With a pious air, Radek describes the false position of the whole leading party stratum as a sort of "accident". But that has little value as a Marxian explanation of the vulgar democratic position of Kamenev, Zinoviev, Stalin, Molotov, Rykov, Kalinin, Nogin, Miliutin, Krestinsky, Frunze, Yaroslavsky, Ordjonikidze, Preobrazhensky, Smilga, and a dozen other "old Bolsheviks". Would it not be more correct to acknowledge that the old algebraic Bolshevik formula contained certain dangers within it: political development might have, as always used to happen with revolutionary formulæ not carried out to the end, filled it with a content hostile to the proletarian revolution. It is self-understood that if Lenin had lived in Russia and had observed the development of the party, day in and day out, especially during the war, he would have given the necessary correctives and interpretations in time. Luckily for the revolution, he arrived soon enough, even though after a delay, to undertake the necessary ideological re-armament. The class instinct of the proletariat and the revolutionary pressure of the lower party strata, prepared by the preceding work of Bolshevism, made it possible for Lenin, in struggle with the leading heads and against them, to switch the policy of the party onto a new track in the shortest period of time.

Does it follow from this that today also we accept for China, India and the other countries Lenin's formula of 1905 in its algebraic inarticulateness, and that we must leave it to the Chinese and Indian Stalins and Rykovs (Tang Pin Shan, Roy and others) to fill the formula with a petty bourgeois national democratic content in order—thereupon to wait for the timely appearance of a Lenin who will undertake the necessary correctives of April 4?   Is such a corrective perhaps assured for China and India?   Or is it not more correct to make the formula right now as concrete as historical experience, in China as well as in Russia, has taught us?

Is what has been stated to be understood as though the slogan of the democratic dictatorship of the proletariat and peasantry was simply a "mistake"? Nowadays, as is known, all ideas and actions of man are divided into two categories: absolutely correct ones, that is, such as fit into the "general line", and absolutely false ones, that is, deviations from this line. This naturally does not prevent what is absolutely correct today from being declared absolutely false tomorrow.   But the real development of ideas also knew, before the emergence of the "general line", the method of successive approaches to the truth.   Even a simple arithmetical division forces the experimental selection of figures, in which one begins either with the large ones or the small ones, in order to reject them at the revision.   In shooting at an object, artillery calls the method of successive approximations, "Bracket". The method of approximation, in politics too, is entirely unavoidable.   The whole question lies only in perceiving in time that a shot fallen short is a shot fallen short and in undertaking the necessary corrective without loss of time.

The greatest historical significance of Lenin's formula lay in the fact that, under the conditions of a new historical epoch, it exhausted one of the most important theoretical and political questions of the day, and that was the question of the attainable level of political independence of the various petty bourgeois groupings, above all, the peasantry. Thanks to its completeness, the Bolshevik experience of 1905-1917 firmly bolted the door against the "democratic dictatorship". With his own hand, Lenin wrote the inscription over this door: Neither entrance nor exit. He formulated it in these words: The peasant goes either with the bourgeois or with the worker. The epigones, however, completely ignore this conclusion to which the old formula of Bolshevism led, and contrary to this conclusion they canonize a provisional hypothesis by inserting it into the program. For it is really in this, generally speaking, that the essence of epigonism lies.

VI

On the Skipping of Historical Stages

*R*ADEK DOES not merely repeat a few official critical writing exercises of recent years, but he over-
simplifies them, in so far as that is possible.   From
his words, it follows that I made no distinction at all
between the bourgeois and the socialist revolutions,
between the East and the West, neither in 1905 nor
today.   Following Stalin, Radek too enlightens me
on the inadmissibility of skipping historical stages.
   Well, then, the question must first of all be put:
If in 1905 it was for me simply a matter of the "socialist revolution", then why did I then believe that it
could begin in backward Russia sooner than in advanced Europe?   Out of patriotism?   In fine, out of
national pride?   And yet that is how it did happen.
Does Radek grasp this: Could the democratic revolution have been realized by us as an *independent* stage,
we would not have had today the dictatorship of the
proletariat.   If it came earlier than in the West, then
it was precisely and only because history united the
main content of the bourgeois revolution with the first
stage of the proletarian revolution—did not mix them
up but united them organically.

To distinguish between the bourgeois and the proletarian revolution is political A B C. But after the A B C follow the syllables, the combination of the letters. History accomplished just such a combination of the most important letters of the bourgeois alphabet with the first letters of the socialist alphabet. Radek, however, would like to drag us back from the first finished syllables to the alphabet. It is sad but true.

It is nonsense to say that stages can never be skipped. The living historical process makes lasting leaps over single "stages" which follow from the theoretical division of the process of evolution in its entirety, that is, in its maximum completeness, and at critical moments demands the same of revolutionary policy. It may be said that the first distinction between a revolutionist and a vulgar evolutionist lies in the capacity to recognize and exploit this moment.

Marx's division of the evolution of industry into handicraft, manufacture and factory is part of the A B C of political economy, or more precisely, of historico-economic theory. In Russia, however, the factory came by skipping over the epoch of manufacture and of urban handicrafts. These are already the syllables of history. A similar process took place in the country in class relationships and politics. The recent history of Russia cannot be comprehended unless the Marxian schema of the three stages is known: handicraft, manufacture, factory. But if one knows *only* this, he still comprehends nothing. For the fact is that the history of Russia—Stalin should not take it to heart—skipped over many stages. The theoretical distinction of the stages, however, is necessary for Russia too, otherwise one can comprehend neither what this leap consisted of nor what the consequence of it was.

The matter can also be approached from another
side (just as Lenin *many times* approached the dual
power), and it can be said that Russia went through
all three of Marx's stages. The first two, however, in
an extremely concentrated form, in embryo, so to say.
These "rudiments", stages of handicraft and manufacture indicated by points, as it were, suffice to confirm
the genetic unity of the economic process. Here, however, the quantitative contraction of the two stages
is so great that it engendered entirely new qualitative
characteristics in the whole social structure of the nation. The most striking expression of this new "quality" in politics is the October revolution.

What is most unbearable in this discussion is the
"theorizing" of Stalin, with the two trinkets which constitute his whole theoretical baggage: "the law of uneven development" and the "non-skipping of stages".
Stalin does not understand to this day that the *skipping of stages* (or remaining too long at one stage)
is just what the uneven development consists of.
Against the theory of the permanent revolution, Stalin,
with inimitable seriousness, sets up . . . the law of
uneven development. Yet, the prognosis that historically backward Russia could arrive at the proletarian
revolution sooner than advanced England, rests entirely upon the law of uneven development. Only, for
this prognosis, one had to understand the historic unevenness in its whole dynamic concreteness, and not
simply be a permanent repeater of a quotation from
Lenin in 1915, which is turned upside down and interpreted in the manner of an illiterate.

The dialectic of the historical "stages" is relatively
easy to understand in periods of revolutionary ascent.
Reactionary periods, on the contrary, naturally and

necessarily become epochs of the cheapest evolutionism. The Staliniad, this gross ideological vulgarity, the worthy daughter of the party reaction, has created a cult of the movement of stages, as a cover for its mechanical repetition and collection of fragments. This reactionary ideology has now been seized upon by Radek, too.

One stage or another of the historical process can prove to be inevitable under certain conditions, although theoretically it does not appear inevitable. And conversely: theoretically "inevitable" stages can be compressed into nothing by the dynamics of development, especially during revolutions, which have not been called the locomotives of history for nothing.

That is how the proletariat, with us, "skipped" the stage of democratic parliamentarism, by only granting the Constituent Assembly a life of hours, and even that only in the backyard of history. But the counter-revolutionary stage in China can in no way be skipped over, just as with us the period of the four Dumas could not be skipped over. The present counter-revolutionary stage in China, however, was historically in no sense "unavoidable". It is the direct result of the catastrophic policy of Stalin-Bucharin, who will pass into history as the organizers of defeats. And the fruits of opportunism have become an objective factor, which can check the revolutionary process for a long time.

Every attempt to skip over real, that is, objectively conditioned stages in the development of the masses, signifies political adventurism. So long as the majority of the working masses have confidence in the social democrats, or let us say, the Kuo Min Tang or the trade unionists, we cannot pose the task of the immediate overthrow of the bourgeois power. The masses must be prepared for that. The preparation can prove to be a very long "stage". But only a *chvostist** can believe that "together with the masses" we must sit, first in the Right and then in the Left Kuo Min Tang, or maintain a bloc with the strike-breaker Purcell, until "the mass is disillusioned with its leaders"—whom we, in the meantime, supported by our friendship and invested with authority.

Radek will hardly have forgotten that many "dialecticians" characterized the demand for withdrawal from the Kuo Min Tang and the break with the Anglo-Russian Committee as nothing but a skipping over of stages, and besides that, as a separation from the peasantry (in China) and from the working masses (in England). Radek ought to remember this all the better since he himself belonged to the "dialecticians" of this sorry type. At the moment, he is only deepening and generalizing his opportunist errors.

In April 1919, Lenin wrote in a programmatic article, *The Third International and Its Place in History:*

"We will hardly go wrong when we say that it was precisely the contradiction between the backwardness of Russia and its *'leap' over bourgeois democracy* to the highest form of democratism—to proletarian or Soviet democracy, that precisely this contradiction was one of the reasons . . . which in the West made especially difficult or retarded the understanding of the rôle of the Soviets." (Lenin, Volume XVI, page 183.)

Lenin says here directly that Russia made a "leap over bourgeois democracy". To be sure, Lenin, even if indirectly, supplemented this contention with all the

* Literally, "tail-endist". One who drags along in tow of events.—Tr.

necessary limitations: the dialectic does not consist of always repeating all the concrete conditions; writers take it for granted that the reader himself also has something in his head. The leap over bourgeois democracy remains in spite of that, and makes difficult, according to the correct observation of Lenin, the understanding of the rôle of the Soviets for all dogmaticians and schematicists—not only in the West, but also in the East.

And in that foreword to the book *1905*, which now suddenly gives Radek so many headaches, it says:

"Already in 1905, the Petersburg workers called their Soviet a proletarian government. This designation passed into the everyday language of that time and completely coincided with the program of the struggle of the working class for power. At the same time, however, *we set up against czarism the elaborated program of political democracy* (universal suffrage, republic, militia, etc.). We could act in no other way. Political democracy is *a necessary stage in the development of the working masses*—with the highly important reservation that in one case this stage lasts for decades, while in the other, the revolutionary situation permits the masses to emancipate themselves from the prejudices of political democracy even before its institutions have been converted into reality." (Trotsky, *1905*, foreword, page 7.)

These words, which, by the by, are in complete accord with the ideas of Lenin quoted by me, sufficiently explain, it seems to me, the necessity of setting up against the dictatorship of the Kuo Min Tang the "elaborated program of political democracy". But it is precisely at this point that Radek attacks from the Left. In the epoch of the revolutionary ascent he resisted the withdrawal of the Chinese Communist

Party from the Kuo Min Tang. In the epoch of the
counter-revolutionary dictatorship, he resists the mobilization of the Chinese workers under the slogan of
democracy. This amounts to wearing furs in summer
and going naked in winter.

VII

What Does the Slogan of the Democratic Dictatorship Mean Today for the East?

STUMBLING INTO the Stalinist—evolutionary philistine, but not revolutionary—conception of the historical "stages", Radek too now endeavors to canonize the slogan of the democratic dictatorship of the proletariat and the peasantry for the whole East. Out of the working hypothesis of Bolshevism, which Lenin adapted to the course of development of a definite country, which he changed, concretized and at a certain stage rejected, Radek makes a supra-historical schema. On this point he persistently repeats the following in his articles:

"This theory, as well as the tactic flowing from it, is applicable to all countries with a young capitalist development, in which the bourgeoisie has not solved the problems which the preceding social-political formations have left behind as a heritage."

Just reflect upon this formula: is it not a solemn justification of Kamenev's position in 1917? Did the Russian bourgeoisie liquidate the problems of the democratic revolution by the February revolution? No,

they remained unsolved, including the most important
of them, the agrarian problem. How could Lenin fail
to comprehend that the old formula was still "applicable"? Why did he withdraw it?

Radek answered us on this point before: because it
had already "been realized". We have examined this
answer. It is completely untenable, doubly untenable
in the mouth of Radek, who holds the view that the
essence of the old Leninist formula does not at all lie
in the forms of power but in the actual liquidation of
serfdom by the collaboration of the proletariat and
the peasantry. But this is precisely what the Kerenskiad did not produce. From this it follows that Radek's excursion into our past for the purpose of solving the most timely question of the day, the Chinese
question, is altogether absurd. It is not what Trotsky understood or failed to understand in 1905 that
should have been investigated, but rather what Stalin,
Molotov and especially Rykov and Kamenev did not
grasp in February-March 1917 (what Radek's position was in those days, I do not know). For if one
believes that the democratic dictatorship was "realized" to such an extent in the dual power as to require a change of the central slogan, then one must
recognize that the "democratic dictatorship" in China
was realized still more completely and more fundamentally through the régime of the Kuo Min Tang,
that is, through the rule of Chiang Kai-Shek and
Wang Chin Wei, with Tang Ping Shan as appendage*.

---

* Chiang Kai-Shek is the leader of the Right wing, and
Wang Chin Wei of the Left wing of the Kuo Min Tang. Tang
Ping Shan was in the leadership of the Communist Party of
China during the revolutionary upsurge, defended the policies
of Stalin-Bucharin-Martinov in China, was one of the spokes-
men in the international campaign against "Trotskyism" and

It was all the more necessary, therefore, to change the slogan of China.

Is then the "heritage of the preceding social-political formations" liquidated in China? No, it is not yet liquidated. But was it liquidated by us on April 4, 1917, when Lenin declared war upon the whole upper stratum of the "old Bolsheviks"? Radek contradicts himself hopelessly, blunders and reels from side to side. Let us remark in this connection that it is not entirely accidental that he uses so complicated and circumlocutory an expression as "heritage of the formations", varied at different passages, and obviously avoids the clearer term: "remnants of feudalism, or of serfdom". Why? Because Radek only yesterday denied these remnants most decisively and thereby tore away any basis for the slogan of the democratic dictatorship. In his report in the Communist Academy, Radek said:

"The resources of the Chinese revolution are no less deep than were the resources of our revolution in 1905. One can assert with certainty that the alliance of the working class with the peasantry will be stronger there than it was with us in 1905, *for the simple reason that it will not be directed against two classes, but only against one, the bourgeoisie.*"

Yes, "for the simple reason". Now, when the proletariat, together with the peasantry, directs itself against one class, the bourgeoisie—not against the remnants of feudalism, but against the bourgeoisie—what—if you please—is such a revolution called? Per-

became the "Communist" minister of agriculture in the bourgeois government of Hankow in 1927. He is now outside the ranks of the Communist Party of China and has since become an adversary of Communism.—Tr.

haps a democratic revolution? Just notice that Radek said this not in 1905, and not even in 1909, but in
March 1927. How is this to be understood? Very
simply. In March 1927, Radek also deviated from the
right road, only in another direction. In its theses
on the Chinese question, the Opposition inserted a most
important correction to Radek's onesidedness of that
time. But in the words just quoted there was nevertheless a kernel of truth: there is almost no class of
landowners in China, the landowners are much more
intimately bound up with the capitalists than in czarist Russia, the specific weight of the agrarian question in China is therefore much lighter than in czarist
Russia; but for that, the question of national liberation occupies a large place. Accordingly, the capacity of the Chinese peasantry for *independent* revolutionary political struggle for the democratic renova-
tion of the country can in no case be greater than
was the Russian peasantry's. This found its expression, among other things, in the fact that neither before 1925 nor during the three years of the revolution
in China, did a people's party arise which inscribed
the agrarian revolution upon its banner. All this
taken together demonstrates that for China, which has
already left behind it the experience of 1925-1927, the
formula of the democratic dictatorship presents a
much more dangerous reactionary snare than in Russia after the February revolution.

Still another excursion by Radek in an even further
distant past, turns just as mercilessly against him.
In this case, it is concerned with the slogan of the permanent revolution which Marx raised in 1850:

"With Marx," writes Radek, "there was no slogan
of a democratic dictatorship, while with Lenin, from
1905 to 1917, it was the political axis, and formed a

component part of his conception of the revolution *in all* [? !] *countries* of a beginning [?] capitalist development."

Basing himself upon a few lines from Lenin, Radek explains this difference of positions by the fact that the central task of the German revolution was *national unification*, while *with us it was the agrarian question*. If this contrast is not mechanized, and due regard is had for proportion, then it is correct up to a certain point. But then what is to happen with China? The specific weight of the national problem in China, a semi-colonial country, is immeasurably greater in comparison with the agrarian problem than it was even in Germany in 1848-1850; for in China it is simultaneously a question of unification as well as of liberation. Marx formulated his perspectives of the permanent revolution when, in Germany, all the thrones still stood firm, the Junkers held the land, and the leaders of the bourgeoisie were tolerated only in the antechamber of the government. In China, there has been no monarchy since 1911, there is no independent landowning class, the national bourgeois Kuo Min Tang is in power, the relationships of serfdom are, so to speak, chemically fused with bourgeois exploitation. The contrast of the positions of Marx and Lenin undertaken by Radek thereby speaks entirely against the slogan of the democratic dictatorship in China.

But Radek does not even take up the position of Marx seriously, only in passing, episodically, confining himself to the circular of 1850, *where Marx still considered the peasantry the natural allies of the petty bourgeois city democracy.* Marx at that time expected the independent stage of the democratic revolution in Germany, that is, the temporary assumption of power by the city petty bourgeois radicals, sup-

ported by the peasantry. There's the rub! That,
however, is just what did not happen. And not accidentally. Already in the middle of the past century,
the petty bourgeois democracy showed itself to be
powerless to carry out its revolution independently.
And Marx took up this lesson in his calculations. On
April 16, 1856—that is, six years after the circular
mentioned—Marx wrote to Engels:

"The whole matter in Germany will depend upon the
possibility of supporting the proletarian revolution
with a sort of second edition of the peasant war. Then
the thing will be excellent."

These splendid words, completely forgotten by Radek, constitute a truly invaluable key to the October
revolution as well as to the whole problem that occupies us here. Did Marx skip over the agrarian
revolution? No, as we see, he did not skip over it.
Did he consider the collaboration of the proletariat
and the peasantry necessary in the next revolution?
Yes, he did. Did he grant the possibility of the leading, or even only the independent rôle of the peasantry
in the revolution? No, he did not grant this possibility. He proceeded from the fact that the peasantry, which had not succeeded in supporting the bourgeois democracy in the independent democratic revolution (through the fault of the bourgeois democracy,
not the peasantry), would be in a position to support
the proletariat in the proletarian revolution. "Then
the thing will be excellent." Radek, however, does not
want to see that this is what happened in October,
and did not happen badly at that.

With regard to China, the conclusions following
from this are quite clear. The dispute is not over the
decisive rôle of the peasantry as an ally, and not over
the great significance of the agrarian revolution, but

over whether an independent agrarian democratic revolution is possible in China or whether "a second edition of the peasant war" will give support to the proletarian revolution.   That is the only way the question
stands.   Whoever puts it differently, has learned nothing and understood nothing, only confuses the Chinese Communist Party and drives it off the right track.

In order for the proletariat of the Eastern countries to open the road to victory, the pedantic reactionary theory of Stalin-Martinov on "stages" and
"steps" must be eliminated at the very outset, must
be   cast   aside, demolished and swept away with a
broom.   Bolshevism grew in the struggle against this
vulgar evolutionism.   It is not to a line of march
marked out *a priori* that we must adapt ourselves, but
to the real course of the class struggle.   Away with
the Stalin-Kuusinen idea: to prescribe a succession for
the countries of various degrees of development, to
apportion them in advance with revolutionary rations
by card.   One must adapt oneself to the real course
of the class struggle.   An inestimable guide for this
is Lenin; only, the *whole* Lenin must be taken into consideration.

When in 1919, Lenin, especially in connection with
the organization of the Communist International, combined into a unit the conclusions out of the period
gone by, and gave it an ever more rounded-out theoretical formulation, he interpreted the experience of the
Kerenskiad and the October as follows: In a bourgeois
society with already developed class antagonisms there
can only be either an open or disguised dictatorship
of the bourgeoisie, or the dictatorship of the proletariat.   There canot be any talk of a transitional
régime.   Every democracy, every "dictatorship of
democracy" (the   ironical   quotation   marks   are

Lenin's) is only a veil for the rule of the bourgeoisie, as the experience of the most backward European country, Russia, showed in the epoch of the bourgeois revolution, that is, in an epoch favorable to the "dictatorship of democracy". This conclusion was taken by Lenin as the basis for his theses on democracy, which arose only as the sum of the experiences of the February and October revolutions.

Like many others, Radek also separates mechanically the question of democracy from the question of the democratic dictatorship in general. The "democratic dictatorship", however, can only be the masked rule of the bourgeoisie in the revolution. This is taught us by the experience of our "dual power" of 1917 as well as by the experience of the Chinese Kuo Min Tang.

The hopelessness of the epigones is most crassly expressed in the fact that even now they still attempt to contrast the democratic dictatorship to the dictatorship of the bourgeoisie, as well as to the dictatorship of the proletariat. But this means that the democratic dictatorship must have a transitional character, that is, a petty bourgeois content. The participation of the proletariat in it does not change the situation, for there is no arithmetical average in nature of the various class lines. If it is neither the dictatorship of the bourgeoisie nor the dictatorship of the proletariat, then it means that the petty bourgeoisie must play the *determining* and *decisive* rôle. But this brings us back to the question to which the three Russian and the two Chinese revolutions have answered in practise: Is the petty bourgeoisie today, under the conditions of the world domination of imperialism, capable of playing a leading revolutionary rôle in the capitalist countries, even when it is a question of backward countries, which are still confronted with the solution of their democratic tasks?

There have been epochs in which the lower strata of the petty bourgeoisie were able to set up their revolutionary dictatorship. That we know. But they were epochs in which the proletariat or prescursors of the proletariat of the time was not distinguished from the petty bourgeoisie, but on the contrary constituted in its undeveloped condition its fighting core. Quite different today. We cannot speak of the ability of the petty bourgeoisie to direct the life of present-day, even if backward, bourgeois society, in so far as the proletariat has separated itself from the petty bourgeoisie and is pitted antagonistically against the big bourgeoisie on the basis of capitalist development, which condemns the petty bourgeoisie to vegetation and puts the peasantry before the political choice between the bourgeoisie and the proletariat. Every time the peasantry seemingly decides for a petty bourgeois party, it actually supports on its back finance capital. If, in the period of the first Russian revolution, or in the period between the first two revolutions, there could still exist differences of opinion over the *degree of independence* (but only the degree!) of the peasantry and the petty bourgeoisie in the democratic revolution, now this question has been decided by the whole course of the events of the last twelve years, and decided irrevocably.

It was raised anew in practise after the October in various countries, and in various forms and combinations, and everywhere it was settled the same way. The most fundamental experience after the Kerenskiad is, as already mentioned, the Kuo Min Tang. But no lesser importance is to be attached to the experiment of Fascism in Italy, where the petty bourgeoisie with arms in hand, snatched the power from the old bourgeois parties in order to surrender immediately, through its leaders, to the financial oligarchy. The same question arose in Poland, where the Pilsudski movement was aimed directly against the reactionary bourgeois landowning government and mirrored the hopes of the petty bourgeois masses and even a wide circle of the proletariat. It is no accident that the old Polish social democrat, Warski, out of fear of "underestimating the peasantry", identified the Pilsudski overthrow with the "democratic dictatorship of the workers and peasants". It would lead us too far afield if I were to analyze here the Bulgarian experiences, that is, the disgraceful policy of confusion of the Kolarovs and Kabaktchievs towards the party of Stambuliski, or the shameful experiment with the Farmer-Labor party in the United States, or Zinoviev's romance with Raditch, or the experiments of the Communist Party of Rumania, and so on and so forth without end. Some of these questions are analyzed in their essential parts in my *Criticism of the Program of the Comintern.* The fundamental conclusion confirms and strengthens completely the lessons of October: The petty bourgeoisie, together with the peasantry, is incapable of the rôle of leader in modern, even if backward, bourgeois society, in revolutionary as well as in reactionary epochs. The peasantry can either support the dictatorship of the bourgeoisie, or serve to prop up the dictatorship of the proletariat. Transitional forms are only a disguise of the dictatorship of the bourgeoisie which has begun to totter or, after a shock, has come to its feet again (Kerenskiad, Fascism, Pilsudski régime).

The peasantry can go either with the bourgeoisie or with the proletariat. But when the proletariat attempts to march at all costs with the peasantry, which does not yet follow it, the proletariat proves inevitably to be in tow of finance capital: workers as defenders of the fatherland in Russia in 1917; workers, including the Communists as well, in the Kuo Min Tang in China; workers, among them the Communists in part as well, in the Polish Socialist Party in Poland in 1926, etc.

Whoever does not think this out to the end, and who has not understood the events from the fresh trail they have left behind, had better not delve into revolutionary politics.

The most fundamental conclusion which Lenin drew from the lessons of the February and the October revolutions, and drew exhaustively and comprehensively, thoroughly rejects the idea of the "democratic dictatorship". The following was repeated by Lenin since 1918 more than once:

"All political economy—if one has learned anything at all from it—the whole history of the revolution, the whole history of political development during the nineteenth century, teaches us that the peasant goes either with the worker or with the bourgeois. If you do not know this, I would like to say to such citizens . . . just reflect upon the development of any one of the great revolutions of the eighteenth or the nineteenth centuries, upon the political history of any country in the nineteenth century. It will tell you why. The economy of capitalist society is such that the ruling power can only be either capital or the proletariat which overthrows it. Other forces there are none in the economics of this society." (Volume XVI, page 217.)

It is not a matter here of modern England or Germany. On the basis of the lessons of any one of the great revolutions of the eighteenth or the nineteenth

centuries, that is, of the *bourgeois* revolutions in the
backward countries, Lenin comes to the conclusion
that only the dictatorship of the bourgeoisie or the
dictatorship of the proletariat is possible.   There cannot be a "democratic", that is, an intermediate dictatorship.

* * *

His theoretical and historical excursion is summed
up by Radek, as we see, in the rather poor aphorism
that the bourgeois revolution must be distinguished
from the socialist.   Sinking down to this "level", Radek straightway stretches out a finger to Kuusinen
who, proceeding from his one lone resource, that is,
"healthy common sense", considers it improbable that
the slogan of the proletarian dictatorship can be raised
in the advanced as well as in the backward countries.
With the candor of a man who understands nothing,
Kuusinen convicts Trotsky of having "learned nothing" since 1905.   Following Kuusinen, Radek also becomes ironical: for Trotsky "the peculiarity of the
Chinese and Indian revolutions consists precisely of
the fact that they are in no way distinguished from
the western European revolutions and must therefore,
in the first steps [? !] lead to the dictatorship of the
proletariat".

Radek forgets one trifle in this connection: The dictatorship of the proletariat was not realized in a
western European country, but precisely in a backward eastern European country. Is it Trotsky's fault
that the historical process overlooked the "peculiarity" of Russia?   Radek forgets further that the bourgeoisie, that is, more precisely expressed, finance capital, rules in *all* the capitalist countries, with all the
multiplicity of the degrees of development of the social
structures,   traditions,   etc.,   that is, with all their

"peculiarity". Here again, the lack of respect for this peculiarity proceeds from the historical development but in no case from Trotsky.

Then wherein lies the distinction between the advanced and the backward countries? The distinction is great, but it still remains within the confines of the domination of capitalist relationships. The forms and methods of the rule of the bourgeoisie differ greatly in different countries. At one pole, the domination bears a stark and absolute character: the *United States*. At the other pole, finance capital adapts itself to the outlived institutions of the Asiatic Middle Ages, by subjecting them to it and imposing its methods upon them: *India*. But the bourgeoisie rules in both places. From this it follows that the dictatorship of the proletariat also will have a highly varied character with regard to the social basis, the political forms, the immediate tasks and the tempo of the work in the various capitalist countries. But to lead the masses of the people to victory over the bloc of the imperialists, the feudal and the national bourgeoisie, can be done only by the revolutionary hegemony of the proletariat, which transforms itself after the seizure of power into the dictatorship of the proletariat.

Radek fancies that when he has divided humanity into two groups: into one which has "matured" for the socialist dictatorship, and into another which has "matured" only for the democratic dictatorship, he has by this alone, in contrast to me, taken into consideration the imaginary "peculiarity" of the individual countries. In reality, he has turned out a lifeless blueprint which can only divert the Communists from a genuine study of the peculiarity of every country. Yet, the correct system of the tasks and actions

of a reliable program of struggle for influence upon
the masses of workers and peasants can arise only
out of the most minute study of the real peculiarity
of a given country, that is, of the living texture of the
levels and stages of historical development.

The peculiarities of a country which has not accomplished or completed its democratic revolution are
of such great significance that they must be taken as
the basis for the program of the proletarian vanguard.
Only upon the basis of such a *national* program can a
Communist party develop its real and successful struggle for the majority of the working class and the
toilers in general against the bourgeoisie and their
democratic agents.

The possibility of success in this struggle is of
course determined to a large extent by the rôle of the
proletariat in the economy of the country, that is, by
the degree of its capitalist development. This, however, is by no means the only criterion. No less important is the question whether so far-reaching and
burning a "problem of the people" exists in the country, in the solution of which the majority of the nation
is interested, and which demands for its solution the
boldest revolutionary measures. To problems of this
kind are counted the agrarian question and the national question, in their most varied combinations.
With the accentuated agrarian problem and with the
insupportability of the national subjugation in the
colonial countries, the young and relatively not num-
erous proletariat can come to power, on the basis of a
national democratic revolution, sooner than the proletariat of an advanced country on the basis of a
purely *socialist* revolution. It would seem that after
the October it would not be necessary to prove this
any more. But through the years of ideological re-

action and through the theoretical depravity of the
epigones, the elementary conceptions of the revolution have become so rank, so putrid and so . . .
Kuusinified, that one is compelled each time to begin
all over again.

Does it follow from what has been said that all
the countries of the world, in one way or another, are
already today ripe for the socialist revolution? No,
this is a false, a dead, scholastic, Stalinist-Bucharin-
ist way of putting the question. World economy in
its entirety is indubitably ripe for socialism. But.
this does not mean that every country individually is.
ripe. Then what is to happen with the dictatorship
of the proletariat in the various backward countries,
in China, India, etc.? To this we answer: History
is not made to order. A country can become "ripe"
for the dictatorship of the proletariat not only before
it is ripe for the independent construction of socialism, but even before it is ripe for far-reaching sociali-
zation measures. One must not proceed from a pre-
conceived harmony of social evolution. The law of
uneven development still lives, despite the tender theoretical embraces of Stalin. The force of this law oper-
ates not only in the relations of countries to each
other, but also in the mutual relationships of the
various processes within a country. A reconciliation
of the uneven processes of economics and politics can
be attained only on a world scale. Especially does
this mean that the question of the dictatorship of the
proletariat in China cannot be considered exclusively
within the limits of Chinese economics and Chinese
politics.

Here we run right up against the two mutually exclusive standpoints: the international revolutionary
theory of the permanent revolution and the national

reformist theory of socialism in one country.   Not
only backward China, but in general, no country in
the world can build up socialism within its own national limits: the highly developed productive forces,
which have grown out beyond the national boundaries,
resist this just as do the forces insufficiently developed
for nationalization.   The dictatorship of the proletariat in England, for example, would encounter difficulties and contradictions, different in character,
it   is   true,   but   not   slighter ones than those that
will offer opposition to the dictatorship of the proletariat in China.   To surmount these contradictions is
possible in both cases only by way of the international
revolution.   This standpoint leaves no room for the
question of the "maturity" or "immaturity" of China
for the socialist transformation.   What remains in-
disputable here is that the backwardness of China
makes the tasks of the proletarian dictatorship extremely difficult.   But we repeat: history is not made
to order, and nobody has placed the Chinese proletariat before a choice.

   Does this at least mean that every country, including the most backward colonial country, is ripe, if not
for socialism, then for the dictatorship of the proletariat?   No, this is not what it means.   Then what is
to happen with the democratic revolution in general—
and in the colonies in particular?   Where is it written—I answer the question with another question—
that every colonial country is ripe for the immediate
and thoroughgoing solution of its national democratic
problems?   The question must be approached from
the other end.   Under the conditions of the imperialist
age, the national democratic revolution can be carried
through to a victorious end only when the social and
political relationships of the country are mature for

putting the proletariat in power as the leader of the
masses of the people.   And if this is not yet the case?
Then the struggle for national liberation will produce
only very partial results, results directed against the
toiling masses.   In 1905, the proletariat of Russia
did not prove to be strong enough to unite the peasant
masses   around it and to conquer   power.   For this
reason, the   revolution   remained standing half way
along the road, and sank deeper and deeper. In China,
where, in spite of the exceptional favorable situation, the leadership of the Communist International
prevented the Chinese proletariat from fighting for
power, the national problems found a miserable, vac-
illating, shabby solution in the régime of the Kuo
Min Tang.

When and under what conditions a colonial country becomes ripe for the real revolutionary solution
of its agrarian and its national problems, cannot be
foretold.   But in any case, we can assert today with
full certainty that not only China, but also India, will
attain genuine popular democracy, that is, workers'
and peasants' democracy, only through the dictatorship of the proletariat.   On that road, many stages,
steps and phases can still arise.   Under the pressure
of the masses of the people, the bourgeoisie will still
take various steps to the Left, in order then to turn all
the more mercilessly against the people.   Periods of
dual power are possible and probable. But what there
will not be, what there cannot be, is a genuine democratic dictatorship that is not the dictatorship of the
proletariat.   An "independent" democratic dictatorship can only be of the type of the Kuo Min Tang,
that is, directed entirely against the workers and the
peasants.   We must understand this at the outset and
teach it to the masses, without hiding the class real-

ities behind abstract formulæ.

Stalin and Bucharin preached that, thanks to the
yoke of imperialism, the bourgeoisie could carry out
the national revolution in China. The attempt was
made. With what results? The proletariat was put
to the sword. Then it was said: the democratic dictatorship is next. The petty bourgeois dictatorship
proved to be a masked dictatorship of capital. By
accident? No. "The peasant goes either with the
worker or with the bourgeois." In the first case, the
dictatorship of the proletariat arises, in the other, the
dictatorship of the bourgeoisie. It would seem that
the Chinese lesson is clear enough, even if studied from
afar. "No," we are answered, "that was only an
abortive attempt, we want to begin everything all over
again and this time set up the 'genuine' democratic
dictatorship." "In what way?" "On the social basis
of the collaboration of the proletariat and the peasantry." It is Radek who presents us with this latest
discovery. But, if you will permit, the Kuo Min Tang
arose on that very same basis: workers and peasants
"together" hauled the chestnuts out of the fire for the
bourgeoisie. Tell us what the political mechanics of
this collaboration will look like. How do you want
to replace the Kuo Min Tang? What parties will
be in power? Name them at least approximately,
hint at them! To this Radek answers (in 1928!) that
only people who are all done for, who are incapable
of understanding the complexity of Marxism, can be
interested in the incidental technical question of which
class will be the horse and which the rider. A Bolshevik must "divert" attention from the political superstructure in favor of the class basis. Come, you
will have your little joke! There has been enough
"diversion"! More than enough! In China, they di-

verted attention from the question of the party expression of the collaboration of the classes, they led the proletariat into the Kuo Min Tang, they were enraptured by the Kuo Min Tang to the point of self-oblivion, they furiously resisted the withdrawal from the Kuo Min Tang, they cringed from political questions of struggle by the repetition of abstract formulæ; and after the bourgeoisie had very concretely broken the skull of the proletariat, they recommend to us: Let us try all over again. And as a beginning, we once more want to "divert" attention from the question of the parties and the revolutionary power. No. These are very poor jokes. We will not allow ourselves to be pulled back again!

All these acrobatics, as we have perceived, are presented in the interest of an alliance of the workers and peasants. Radek warns the Opposition against an underestimation of the peasantry and recalls the struggle of Lenin against the Mensheviks. If one considers all the things that are contrived with Lenin's quotations, it is often enough to make one sick. Yes, Lenin said more than once that the denial of the revolutionary rôle of the peasantry is characteristic of the Mensheviks. And that was right. But besides these quotations, there nevertheless did come the year 1917, in which the Mensheviks spent the eight months which separated the February from the October revolution, in a firm bloc with the Social Revolutionists. In that period, however, the Social Revolutionists represented the overwhelming majority of the peasantry awakened by the revolution. Together with the S. R.s, the Mensheviks called themselves the revolutionary democracy and remonstrated with us that they were the very ones who based themselves upon the alliance of the workers with the peasants (soldiers). Accord-

ingly, the Mensheviks, so to speak, expropriated the
Bolshevik formula of the alliance of the workers and
peasants after the February revolution. The Bolsheviks were accused by them of wanting to split the
proletarian vanguard from the peasantry and thereby
to destroy the revolution. In other words, the Mensheviks accused Lenin of ignoring, or at least, of underestimating the peasantry.

The criticism of Kamenev, Zinoviev and others
against Lenin was only an echo of the criticism of the
Mensheviks. The present criticism of Radek in turn
is only a belated echo of the criticism of Kamenev.

The policy of the epigones in China, including the
policy of Radek, is the continuation and the further
development of the Menshevik masquerade of 1917.
The fact that the Communist party remained in the
Kuo Min Tang was defended not only by Stalin, but
also by Radek, with the same reference to the necessity of the alliance of the workers and peasants. But
when it was "accidentally" shown that the Kuo Min
Tang was a bourgeois party, the attempt was repeated
with the "Left" Kuo Min Tang. The results were the
same. Thereupon, the abstraction of the democratic
dictatorship, in distinction from the dictatorship of
the proletariat, was elevated above this sorry reality
which had not fulfilled the high hopes. A new repetition of what we already had. In 1917, we heard a
hundred times from Tseretelli, Dan and the others:
"We have the dictatorship of the revolutionary democracy, but you are driving towards the dictatorship
of the proletariat, that is, towards destruction." In
truth, people have short memories. The "revolutionary democratic dictatorship" of Stalin and Radek is
in no way distinguished from the "dictatorship of the
revolutionary democracy" of Tseretelli and Dan. And

in spite of that, this formula not only runs through all the resolutions of the Comintern, but it has also penetrated into its program.   It is hard to conceive a more cunning masquerade and at the same time a more bitter revenge of Menshevism for the affronts which Bolshevism heaped upon it in 1917.

The revolutionists of the East, however, still have the right to demand a concrete answer to the question of the character of the "democratic dictatorship", based not upon old, *a priori* quotations, but upon facts and upon political experience.   To the question: What is a "democratic dictatorship"?—Stalin has repeatedly given the truly classic reply: For the East, for example, it is the same as "Lenin conceived it with regard to the 1905 revolution".   This has become the official formula to a certain extent.   It can be found in the books and resolutions devoted to China, India or Polynesia.   Revolutionists are referred to Lenin's "conceptions" concerning future events, which in the meantime have long ago become *past* events, and in addition, the hypothetical "conceptions" of Lenin are one-sidedly and crookedly interpreted, at all events, not in the way that Lenin himself construed them *after* the events.

"All right," says the Communist of the East, hanging his head, "we will try to conceive of it exactly as Lenin, according to your words, conceived of it before the revolution.   But won't you please tell us what this slogan looks like in actuality?   How was it realized with you?"

"With us, it was realized as the Kerenskiad in the epoch of the dual power."

"Can we tell our workers that the slogan of the democratic dictatorship will be realized by us as a national Kerenskiad?"

"Come, come! Not at all! No worker will adopt such a slogan: the Kerenskiad is lackeydom before the bourgeoisie and a betrayal of the toilers."

"But how, then, must we say it to our workers?" the Communist of the East asks sadly.

"You must say," impatiently answers the sentinel Kuusinen, "that the democratic dictatorship is the one that Lenin conceived of with regard to the future democratic revolution."

If the Communist of the East is not lacking in a certain thoughtfulness, he will seek to rejoin:

"But didn't Lenin declare in 1918 that the democratic dictatorship first found its genuine and true realization in the October revolution through the setting up of the dictatorship of the proletariat? Would it not be better to orientate the party and the working class towards this perspective?"

"Under no circumstances. Do not even dare to think about it. Why, that is the per-r-r-manent r-r-r-evolution! That's Tr-r-r-otskyism!"

After this harsh reprimand the Communist of the East turns paler than the snow on the highest peaks of the Himalayas and abandons any further craving for knowledge. Let come what may!

And the consequences? We know them well: either contemptible grovelling before Chiang Kai-Shek, or heroic adventures.

VIII

From Marxism to Pacifism

WHAT IS PERHAPS most disquieting, sympto-
matically, is a passage in Radek's article
which, as it were, stands apart from the central theme
that interests us, but which is intimately bound up with
this theme by the uniformity of Radek's shift towards
the present theoreticians of Centrism.   It is a question of the somewhat disguised advances towards the
theory of socialism in one country.   One must dwell
on this, for this "sideline" of Radek's errors can sur-
pass all the other differences of opinion in its further
development, and it may transpire that its quantity
has in the end turned into quality.

It is a question of the dangers that threaten the
revolution from without.   Radek writes that Lenin

". . . was conscious of the fact *that with the degree of the economic development of Russia in 1905*
this [the proletarian] dictatorship can maintain itself
only if the western European proletariat comes to its
aid."   (My emphasis.   L. T.)

One mistake after another, above all, a very crude
violation of the historical perspective.   In reality
Lenin said, and that more than once, that the dem-

ocratic dictatorship (but not the proletarian) in Russia would be unable to maintain itself without the socialist revolution in Europe. This thought runs like a
thread through all the articles and speeches of Lenin
in the days of the Stockholm party convention in 1906
(polemic against Plechanov, questions of the nationalization of the land, dangers of the restoration, etc.).
In that period, Lenin did not even raise the question
of a proletarian dictatorship in Russia before the socialist revolution in western Europe. But it is not
there that the most imporant thing lies for the moment. What is the meaning of "with the degree of the
economic development of Russia in 1905"? And how
do matters stand with the degree of 1917? It is on
this difference in degree that the theory of socialism
in one country is erected. The program of the Comintern has divided the whole globe into squares which are
"adapted" to the independent construction of socialism and those which are "not adapted", and has thereby created the revolutionary strategy of a series of
hopeless blind alleys. The difference in economic degree can undoubtedly be of decisive significance for
the political power of the working class. In 1905,
we could not raise ourselves to the dictatorship of the
proletariat, just as for that matter, we were unable
to rise to the democratic dictatorship. In 1917, we
set up the dictatorship of the proletariat which embraced the democratic dictatorship. But with the
economic degree of development of 1917, as well as
with the economic degree of 1905, the dictatorship
can maintain itself and develop to socialism only when
the western European proletariat comes opportunely
to its assistance. It is obvious that this "opportune-
ness" cannot be calculated in advance: it is determined
by the course of development and the struggle. As

against this *fundamental* question, determined by the *international* relation of forces which have the last and decisive word, the difference in degree of development of Russia in 1905 and in 1917, however important it is in itself, is a factor of secondary order.

But Radek does not content himself with the ambiguous reference to this difference of degree. After he has referred to the fact that Lenin saw the connection of the inner problems of the revolution with its world problems (Indeed!), Radek adds:

"Lenin did not sharpen the conception of this connection between the maintenance of the socialist dictatorship in Russia and the aid of the western European proletariat through the *excessively accentuated formulation* of Trotsky, namely, that it must be a *state* aid, that is, the aid of the already victorious western European proletariat." (My emphasis. L. T.)

Frankly, I did not trust my eyes when I read these lines. To what end did Radek require this worthless weapon from the arsenal of the epigones? This is really nothing more than a stale reproduction of the Stalinist banalities, which we always used to make such thorough game of. Outside of everything else, the quotation shows that Radek has a very bad notion of the fundamental landmarks of the Leninist path. Lenin, unlike Stalin, never contrasted the pressure of the European proletariat upon the bourgeois power to the capture of power by the proletariat; on the contrary, he formulated the question of revolutionary aid from without much more sharply than I. In the epoch of the first revolution, he repeated tirelessly that we would not retain the democracy (even the democracy!) without the socialist revolution in Europe. In 1917-1918 and the years that followed, Lenin did not consider and estimate the fate of our revolution

in general in any way other than in connection with
the socialist revolution that had begun in Europe. He
asserted openly, for example: "Without the victory of
the revolution in Germany, we are doomed." He said
this in 1918, that is, *not* with the "economic degree of
development" of 1905, and he did not mean future
decades, but the shortest periods, which were to be
measured by a few years if not by months.

Lenin declared dozens of times: if we have held out,
"then only because a *special* combination of circumstances has protected us from international imperialism for a brief moment [for a brief moment! L. T.]".
And further: "International imperialism . . . can in
no way and under no circumstances come to terms with
a Soviet republic existing by its side . . . A conflict
becomes inevitable." And the conclusion? Is it anything like the pacifist hope in the "pressure" of the
proletariat or in the "neutralization" of the bourgeoisie? No, the conclusion reads: "Here lies the
greatest difficulty of the Russian revolution . . . the
need of bringing about the international revolution."
(Volume XV, page 126.) When was this said and
written? Not in 1905, when Nicholas II negotiated
with Wilhelm II on the suppression of the revolution,
and when I advanced my "accentuated" formula, but
in 1918, 1919 and later.

The following is what Lenin said in retrospect at the
Third Congress of the Comintern:

"It was clear to us that the victory of the proletarian revolution [in Russia. L. T.] is impossible without the support of the international revolution, the
world revolution. Even before the revolution, and
also after it, we believed: the revolution will begin immediately, or at least very soon, in the other, capital-
istically advanced countries, otherwise we are lost. And

although we were aware of this, we did everything to maintain the Soviet system under all circumstances and at any price, for we knew that we are working not only for ourselves but also for the international revolution. We knew it, and repeatedly expressed this conviction of ours before the October revolution as well as immediately afterward and during the conclusion of the Brest-Litovsk peace. *And generally speaking this was right.* In reality, the movement did not go in such a straight line as we had expected." (*Minutes of the Third Congress of the Comintern,* page 354, Russian edition.)

Since 1921, the movement began to proceed in a line that was not so straight as we had expected in 1917-1919 (and not only in 1905). But it nevertheless did develop along the line of the irreconcilable antagonism between the workers' state and the bourgeois world. One of the two must perish! To preserve the workers' state from the deadly dangers, not only military but also economic, can be done only by the victorious development of the proletarian revolution in the West. The attempt to discover two positions in this question, Lenin's and mine, is the height of theoretical slovenliness. At least read over Lenin, do not calumniate him, do not feed us with stale Stalinist pap!

But the decline does not come to a halt here. After Radek has invented the story that Lenin considered the "simple" (in essence, reformist, Purcellian) aid of the world proletariat sufficient, while Trotsky "exaggeratedly" demanded the state, that is, revolutionary aid, Radek continues:

"Experience showed *in this* point too that Lenin remained right. The European proletariat was not yet able to capture power, but it was strong enough, during the intervention, to prevent the world bourge-

oisie from throwing strong forces against us.   By that
it helped us maintain the Soviet power.   Fear of the
labor movement, next to the antagonisms in the capitalist world itself, was the main force that guaranteed
the maintenance of peace during the eight years after
the termination of the intervention."

This passage, while it does not sparkle with originality on the background of the writing exercises of the
present-day literary officialdom, is nevertheless noteworthy for its combination of historical anachronism,
political confusion and the grossest errors in principle.

From Radek's words it would follow that Lenin in
1905 foretold in his brochure *Two Tactics* (this is
the only work to which Radek refers) that the relationship of forces between states and classes after
1917 would be such as to exclude for a long time the
possibility of a great military intervention against us.
In contrast to this, Trotsky in 1905 did not foresee
the situation that would necessarily arise after the
imperialist war, but only reckoned with the realities
of that time, such as the mighty Hohenzollern army,
the very strong Hapsburg military power, the almighty
Paris Bourse, etc.   This is a truly monstrous anachronism, which becomes even more complicated by its
ridiculous inner contradictions.   For according to Radek, my principal mistake consisted precisely of the
fact that I did advance the perspective of the dictatorship of the proletariat "with the degree of development of 1905".   Now the second "mistake" becomes
plain: I did not consider the perspective of the dictatorship of the proletariat put forward by me on the
eve of the 1905 revolution in the light of the international situation as it arose after 1917. When the usual
arguments of Stalin look like this, we don't wonder
about it, for we know well enough his "degree of dev-

elopment" in 1917 as well as in 1928.   But how did Radek fall into such company?

Yet even this is not yet the worst.   The worst lies in the fact that Radek has skipped over the boundary that separates Marxism from opportunism, the revolutionary from the pacifist position.   It is a question of nothing less than the struggle against war, that is, of *how and with what methods war can be averted or an end be put to it: by the pressure of the proletariat upon the bourgeoisie or by the civil war to overthrow the bourgeoisie?*   Radek has accidentally introduced the essential question of proletarian policy into this contested field.

Would Radek say that I "ignore" not only the peasantry but also the pressure of the proletariat upon the bourgeoisie, and have taken into consideration the proletarian revolution exclusively?   It is hardly to be assumed that he will defend such an absurdity, worthy of a Thälmann, Semard or a Monmousseau.   At the Third Congress of the Comintern, the ultra-Lefts of that time (Zinoviev, Thalheimer, Thälmann, Bela Kun, etc.) advocated the tactic of putschism in the West as the way to save the U. S. S. R.   Together with Lenin, I explained to them as popularly as possible that it would be the best aid on their part if they would planfully and systematically secure their positions, and prepare themselves for the capture of power, instead of improvising revolutionary adventures for us.   At that time, regrettably enough, Radek was not on the side of Lenin and Trotsky, but on the side of Zinoviev and Bucharin.   But Radek surely recollects—at any rate, the minutes of the Third Congress recollect it—that the essence of the argumentation of Lenin and myself consisted precisely of assailing the irrationally "accentuated formula-

tion" of the ultra-Lefts. After we explained to them
that the strengthening of the party and the growing
pressure of the proletariat is a very serious factor in
internal and international relations, we Marxists added
that "pressure" is a function of the revolutionary
struggle for power and depends entirely upon the
development of the latter. For this reason, Lenin delivered a speech at the end of the Third Congress, at
an enlarged intimate conference of the delegates, which
was directed against the tendencies of passivity and
temporizing, and closed with approximately the following moral: No adventures, but, dear friends, just
the same, hasten a little, for by "pressure" alone we
cannot last long.

Radek refers to the fact that the European proletariat was not in a position to assume power after the
war, but that it prevented the bourgeoisie from beat-
ing us down. We too took the occasion more than
once to speak of this; nevertheless, the European proletariat succeeded in preventing our demolition only
because the pressure of the proletariat coincided with
the heaviest objective consequences of the imperialist
war and the world antagonisms accentuated by them.
Which of these elements was of more decisive significance: the struggle within the imperialist camp, the
economic collapse, or the pressure of the proletariat,
is hard to say, but the question cannot be posed that
way, either. That peaceful pressure alone is inade-
quate was demonstrated too clearly by the imperialist
war, which came in spite of all "pressure". And finally, and this is most important, if the pressure of the
proletariat in the first critical years for the Soviet republic, proved to be effective enough, then it was only
because it was not a question at that time for the
workers of Europe of pressure, but of the struggle

for power, in which this struggle repeatedly assumed the form of civil war.

In 1905, there was neither a war nor an economic collapse in Europe, and capitalism and militarism were distinguished by a raging blood-thirstiness. The "pressure" of the social democracy of that time did not have the power to prevent Wilhelm II or Franz Josef from marching into the kingdom of Poland with their troops, or, in general, to come to the aid of the czar. But even in 1918, the pressure of the German proletariat did not prevent the Hohenzollerns from occupying the Baltic provinces and the Ukraine, and if they did not get as far as Moscow then it was only because their military forces were not adequate. Otherwise why did we conclude the Brest peace? How lightly the yesterdays are forgotten! Without confining himself to the hope in the "pressure" of the proletariat, Lenin repeatedly asserted that without the German revolution we would certainly be destroyed. This was correct in essence, although the intervals were shifted. We need no illusions: we have received an undated moratorium. We live, as before, under the conditions of a "breathing space".

A condition in which the proletariat has not yet seized power, but can prevent the bourgeoisie from utilizing its power for a war, is a condition of a shaky class equilibrium in its sharpest expression. It is just the kind of condition that cannot last long. The scales must dip towards one side or the other. Either the proletariat comes to power, or else the bourgeoisie, by a series of successive blows, weakens the revolutionary pressure in such a way that it once more gains freedom of action, above all in the question of war and peace.

Only a reformist can picture the pressure of the

proletariat upon the bourgeois state as a permanently
increasing factor and as a guarantee against intervention. It is precisely out of this conception that arose
the theory of the construction of socialism in one
country by means of the *neutralization* of the world
bourgeoisie (Stalin). Just as the owl takes flight at
twilight, so also did the Stalinist theory of the neutralization of the bourgeoisie by the pressure of the
proletariat arise only when the conditions which engendered this theory began to disappear.

While the falsely interpreted experience of the post-
war period led to the deceptive hope—we can manage
to live without the revolution of the European proletariat, and substitute for it "support in general"—the
world situation has in the meantime undergone abrupt
changes. The defeats of the proletariat opened up
roads for capitalist stabilization. The collapse of
capitalism after the war was checked. New genera-
tions grew up who had not tasted the horrors of the
imperialist slaughter. The result is that the bourgeoisie is now able to dispose more freely of its war
machine than it was five or eight years ago.

The Leftward radicalization of the working masses
will undoubtedly, in its further development, once more
sharpen the pressure upon the bourgeois state. But
this is a two-edged sword. It is precisely the growing danger from the side of the working class that can,
at a later stage, drive the bourgeoisie to decisive steps
in order to show that it is master at home, and to attempt to destroy the great center of contagion, the
Soviet republic. *The struggle against war is decided
not by pressure upon the government but by the revolutionary struggle for power.* The "pacifist" effects
of the proletarian class struggle, like its reformist
effects, are only by-products of the revolutionary

struggle for power, they have only a relative strength
and can easily turn into the opposite, that is, they
can drive the bourgeoisie on to the road of war.   The
bourgeoisie's fear of the labor movement, to which
Radek refers so one-sidedly, is the most substantial
hope of all social pacifists.   But "fear" of the revolution alone decides nothing.   The revolution decides.
For this reason, Lenin said in 1905 that the only guarantee against the monarchist restoration, and, in 1918,
against the restoration of capitalism, is not the pressure of the proletariat but its revolutionary victory in
Europe.   This is the only correct way of posing the
question.   In spite of the lengthy character of this
"breathing space", it still remains fully in force today.
I too put the question in the very same way.   I wrote
in *Results and Perspectives* in 1906:

"It is precisely the fear of the uprising of the proletariat that compels the bourgeois parties, which vote
fabulous sums for war purposes, to demonstrate sol-
emnly for peace, to dream of international peace institutions, even of the creation of the United States
of Europe—a pitiful declamation which, naturally,
can prevent neither the antagonism between the states
nor armed conflicts." (*Our Revolution, Results and
Perspectives*, page 283.)

The basic mistake of the Sixth Congress consists of
the fact that, in order to save the pacifist and national
reformist perspectives of Stalin-Bucharin, it embarked
upon revolutionary-technical recipes against the war
danger in which it separates the struggle against war
from the struggle for power.

The inspirers of the Sixth Congress, by their very
nature frightened pacifists, terrified constructors of
socialism in one country, made the attempt to perpet-
uate the "neutralization" of the bourgeoisie with the

aid of the strengthened methods of "pressure". But
since they were aware that their leadership up to now
in a series of countries led to the defeat of the revolution, and threw the international vanguard of the
proletariat far back, they endeavored first of all to
square their accounts with the "accentuated formulation" of Marxism, which ties up the problem of war
into an inseparable knot with the problem of the revolution.   They have made the struggle against the
war an independent task.   In order that the national
parties shall not oversleep the decisive hour, they proclaimed the war danger as permanent, unpostponable
and immediate.   Everything that happens in the world
happens for the purpose of war.   War is now no
longer a means of the bourgeois régime, but the bourgeois régime is a means of war.   As a consequence,
the struggle of the Communist International against
war is converted into a system of ritualistic formulæ,
which are repeated automatically at every occasion
and, losing their effectiveness, evaporate.   Stalinist
national socialism has the tendency to convert the
Communist International into an auxiliary means of
"pressure" upon the bourgeoisie.   It is just this tendency, and not Marxism, that helps Radek with his
superficial, draggle-tailed and thoughtless criticism.
He has lost the compass and has landed in a strange
stream that can bring him to far different shores.
ALMA-ATA, *October 1928*

IX

Epilogue

*T*HE PROPHECY or the apprehension which is expressed in the concluding lines of the previous chapter was, as is known, confirmed a few months later. The criticism of the permanent revolution only served Radek as a jumping board to get away from the Opposition. Our whole brochure proves, we hope, that Radek's passage into the camp of Stalin did not come to us unexpectedly. But even renegacy has its gradations, its levels of debasement. In his declaration of repentance, Radek completely rehabilitates Stalin's policy in China. This means to sink down to the level of betrayal. There only remains for me to quote an extract from my reply to the penitent declaration of Radek, Preobrazhensky and Smilga, which is a license for all political cynicism:

"As was seemly for all who set some store by themselves, the trio could not forbear from taking cover behind the permanent revolution. The most tragic experience of the whole recent history of the defeats of opportunism—the Chinese revolution—the trio of capitulators seeks to do away with by the cheap oath that it has nothing in common with the theory of the permanent revolution.

"Radek and Smilga obstinately defended the sub-ordination of the Chinese Communist Party to the bourgeois Kuo Min Tang, not only up to the *coup d'État* of Chiang Kai-Shek but also afterwards. Preo-brazhensky mumbled something incomprehensible, as he always does in political questions. A remarkable fact: all those in the ranks of the Opposition who defended the subordination of the Communist party to the Kuo Min Tang turned out to be capitulators. This outright mark of shame does not burden a single Oppositionist who has remained true to his banner. Seventy-five years after the appearance of the *Com-munist Manifesto*, a quarter of a century after the founding of the party of the Bolsheviks, these ill-starred 'Marxists' considered it possible to defend the remaining of the Communists in the cage of the Kuo Min Tang! In his answer to my charges, Radek al-ready then, just as in his letter of repentance today, frightened us with the 'isolation' of the proletariat from the peasantry in the event that the Communist party withdrew from the bourgeois Kuo Min Tang. Shortly before that, Radek called the Canton govern-ment a peasants' and workers' government and thereby helped Stalin to disguise the subordination of the proletariat to the bourgeoisie. With what are these shameful deeds, the consequences of this blindness, this stupidity, this betrayal of Marxism to be cov-ered? With what? With the permanent revolution!

"As far back as February 1928, Radek, who was already looking for an occasion for his capitulation, adhered promptly to the resolution of the February Plenum of the Executive Committee of the Comintern in 1928 on the Chinese question. This resolution brands the Trotskyists as liquidators because they called defeats, defeats, and were not willing to consider the victorious Chinese counter-revolution as the highest level of the Chinese revolution. In this February resolution the course towards the armed uprising and the Soviets was proclaimed. For every person not devoid of political instinct, sharpened by revolutionary experience, this resolution constitutes a model of the most revolting and most irresponsible adventurism. Radek adhered to it. Preobrazhensky approached the matter no less ingeniously than Radek, only from a different angle. The Chinese revolution, he wrote, is already defeated, and defeated for a long time. A new revolution will not come so soon. Does it pay to squabble about China with the Centrists? On this theme, Preobrazhensky sent out lengthy epistles. When I read them in Alma-Ata, I experienced a feeling of shame. What did these people learn in Lenin's school, I asked myself over and over again. Preobrazhensky's premises were diametrically opposed in content to Radek's premises, yet the conclusions were the same: both of them were inspired by the great desire for Yaroslavsky to embrace them fraternally through the medium of Menzhinsky*. Oh, of course, for the good of the revolution. These are in no sense careerists— heaven forbid: they are simply helpless, ideologically desolated people.

"Against the adventurist resolution of the February Plenum of the E. C. C. I. (1928) I already then put forward the course towards the mobilization of the Chinese workers under the slogan of democracy, including also the Chinese Constituent As-

---

* Menzhinsky is the head of the O. G. P. U., [the State Political Administration]; Yaroslavsky is one of the heads of the Central Control Commission of the party and was especially active in attacking the Opposition and expelling many of its adherents from the party.—Tr.

sembly. But here the hapless trio threw a somersault to the Left: that was cheap and obligated them
to nothing. Democratic slogans? Never. 'This is
a gross mistake of Trotsky.' Chinese Soviets—and
not one percent discount! It is hard to conceive of
anything more senseless than this—by your leave—
position. The slogan 'Soviets!' in the epoch of the
bourgeois reaction is a baby-rattle, a mockery of the
Soviets. But even in the epoch of the revolution, that
is, in the epoch of the direct building of the Soviets,
we did not eliminate the slogans of democracy. We
did not eliminate them until the real Soviets, which had
already conquered power, clashed before the eyes of
the masses with the real institutions of the democracy.
This signifies in the language of Lenin (and not of the
philistine Stalin and his parrots): not to skip over the
democratic stage in the development of the country.

"Outside of the democratic program—constituent
assembly; eight-hour day; confiscation of the land;
national independence of China; right of self-deter-
mination for the peoples living within it—outside of
this democratic program, the Communist Party of
China is bound hand and foot and is compelled to surrender the field passively to the Chinese social democracy which, with the aid of Stalin, Radek and company, would be in a position to assume the place of
the Communist party.

"Thus: although in the tow of the Opposition, Radek nevertheless overslept what was most important in
the Chinese revolution, for he defended the subordination of the Communist party to the bourgeois Kuo Min
Tang. Radek overslept the Chinese counter-revolution, by supporting the course upon the armed uprising after the Canton adventure. Radek today skips
over the   period of the counter-revolution and the

struggle for democracy when, with a defensive gesture, he substitutes for the tasks of the transition period the abstract idea of Soviets beyond time and place. But for that Radek swears that he has nothing in common with the permanent revolution. That is gratifying. That is consoling. . . .

"The anti-Marxian theory of Stalin-Radek contains for China, India and all the countries of the East, the altered but not improved repetition of the Kuo Min Tang experiment.

"On the basis of all the experience of the Russian and Chinese revolutions, on the basis of the teachings of Marx and Lenin, tested in the light of these revolutions, the Opposition contends:

"that the new Chinese revolution can overthrow the existing régime and transfer the power to the masses of the people exclusively in the form of the dictatorship of the proletariat;

"that the 'democratic dictatorship of the proletariat and the peasantry', in contrast to the dictatorship of the proletariat which leads the peasantry and realizes the program of democracy—is a fiction, self-deception, or what is worse yet—a Kerenskiad or a Kuo Min Tang adventure.

"Between the régime of Kerensky and Chiang Kai Shek on the one hand and the dictatorship of the proletariat on the other, there is no revolutionary transitional régime and there can be none; whoever contends anything else is shamefully deceiving the workers of the East and is preparing new catastrophes.

"The Opposition says to the workers of the East: through inner-party machinations, desolated capitulators are helping Stalin to sow the seeds of Centrism, to blind your eyes, to stop up your ears, to befuddle your heads. On the one hand, you are weakened in

face of the naked bourgeois dictatorship by being for-
bidden to unfold the struggle for democracy; on the
other hand, perspectives are painted for you of some
kind of a non-proletarian dictatorship that will deliver you, and thereby new transformations of the
Kuo Min Tang are supported, that is, new suppres-
sions of the workers' and peasants' revolution.

"Such preachers are betrayers. Learn to distrust
them, workers of the East, learn to despise them, learn
to drive them out of your ranks! . . . "

X

What Is the Permanent Revolution?

Fundamental Theses

I HOPE THAT the reader will not object if, to end up this book, I attempt, without fear of repetition, to formulate briefly the most fundamental conclusions.

1. The theory of the permanent revolution now demands the greatest attention of every Marxist, for the course of the ideological and class struggle has finally and conclusively raised this question from the realm of reminiscences over the old differences of opinion among Russian Marxists and converted it into a question of the character, the inner coherence and the methods of the international revolution in general.

2. With regard to the countries with a belated bourgeois development, especially the colonial and semi-colonial countries, the theory of the permanent revolution signifies that the complete and genuine solution of their tasks, *democratic and national emancipation,* is conceivable only through the dictatorship of the proletariat as the leader of the subjugated nation, above all of its peasant masses.

3. Not only the agrarian, but also the national
question, assigns to the peasantry, the overwhelming
majority of the population of the backward countries,
an important place in the democratic revolution. Without an alliance of the proletariat with the peasantry,
the tasks of the democratic revolution cannot be
solved, nor even seriously posed. But the alliance of
these two classes can be realized in no other way than
through an intransigeant struggle against the influence of the national liberal bourgeoisie.

4. No matter how the first episodic stages of the
revolution may be in the individual countries, the realization of the revolutionary alliance between the proletariat and the peasantry is conceivable only under
the political direction of the proletarian vanguard,
organized in the Communist party. This in turn
means that the victory of the democratic revolution
is conceivable only through the dictatorship of the
proletariat which bases itself upon the alliance with
the peasantry and first solves the problems of the democratic revolution.

5. The old slogan of Bolshevism—"the democratic
dictatorship of the proletariat and peasantry" expresses precisely the above characterized relationship
of the proletariat, the peasantry and the liberal bourgeoisie. This has been confirmed by the experience of
October. But the old formula of Lenin does not set-
tle in advance the problem of what the mutual relations between the proletariat and the peasantry inside
of the revolutionary bloc will be. In other words, the
formula has unknown algebraic quantities which have
to make way for precise arithmetical quantities in the
process of historical experience. The latter showed,
and under circumstances that exclude every other interpretation, that no matter how great the revolution-

ary rôle of the peasantry may be, it can nevertheless
not be an independent rôle and even less a leading one.
The peasant follows either the worker or the bourgeois.
This means that the "democratic dictatorship of the
proletariat and peasantry" is only conceivable as a
*dictatorship of the proletariat that leads the peasant
masses behind it.*

6. A democratic dictatorship of the proletariat
and peasantry, as a régime that is distinguished from
the dictatorship of the proletariat by its class content,
might be realized only in case an *independent* revolutionary party could be constituted which expresses the
interests of the peasants and in general of petty-bour-
geois democracy—a party that is capable of conquering power with this or that aid of the proletariat and
of determining its revolutionary program. As modern history teaches—especially the history of Russia
in the last twenty-five years—an insurmountable obstacle on the road to the creation of a peasants' party
is the economic and political dependence of the petty
bourgeoisie and its deep internal differentiation, thanks
to which the upper sections of the petty bourgeoisie
(the peasantry) go with the big bourgeoisie in all
decisive cases, especially in war and in revolution, and
the lower sections—with the proletariat, while the intermediate section has the choice between the two extreme poles. Between the Kerenskiad and the Bolshevik
power, between the Kuo Min Tang and the dictatorship of the proletariat there cannot and does not lie
any intermediate stage, that is, no democratic dictatorship of the workers and peasants.

7. The endeavor of the Comintern to foist upon the
Eastern countries the slogan of the democratic dictatorship of the proletariat and peasantry, finally and
long ago exhausted by history, can have only a reac-

tionary effect. In so far as this slogan is counterposed to the slogan of the dictatorship of the proletariat, it contributes to the dissolution of the
proletariat into the petty bourgeois masses and in this
manner creates better conditions for the hegemony of
the national bourgeoisie and consequently for the collapse of the democratic revolution. The introduction
of this slogan into the program of the Comintern is a
direct betrayal of Marxism and of the October traditions of Bolshevism.

8. The dictatorship of the proletariat which has
risen to power as the leader of the democratic revolution is inevitably and very quickly placed before tasks
that are bound up with deep inroads into the rights of
bourgeois property. The democratic revolution grows
over immediately into the socialist, and thereby becomes a *permanent* revolution.

9. The conquest of power by the proletariat does
not terminate the revolution, but only opens it. Socialist construction is conceivable only on the foundation of the class struggle, on a national and international scale. This struggle, under the conditions of
an overwhelming predominance of capitalist relationships on the world arena, will inevitably lead to ex-
plosions, that is, internally to civil wars, and externally
to revolutionary wars. Therein lies the permanent
character of the socialist revolution as such, regardless of whether it is a backward country that is involved, which only yesterday accomplished its democratic revolution, or an old capitalist country, which
already has behind it a long epoch of democracy and
parliamentarism.

10. The completion of the socialist revolution within
national limits is unthinkable. One of the basic reasons
for the crisis in bourgeois society is the fact that the

productive forces created by it conflict with the framework of the national state. From this follow, on the one hand, imperialist wars, and on the other, the utopia of the bourgeois United States of Europe. The socialist revolution commences on the national arena, is developed further on the inter-state and finally on the world arena. Thus, the socialist revolution becomes a permanent revolution in a newer and broader sense of the word; it attains completion only in the final victory of the new society on our entire planet.

11. The above outlined schema of the development of the world revolution eliminates the question of the countries that are "mature" or "immature" for socialism in the spirit of that pedantic, lifeless classification given by the present program of the Comintern. In so far as capitalism has created the world market, the division of labor and productive forces throughout the world, it has also prepared world economy for socialist transformation.

The various countries will go through this process at different tempos. Backward countries, under certain conditions, can arrive at the dictatorship of the proletariat sooner than the advanced countries, but they come later than the latter to socialism.

A backward colonial or semi-colonial country, whose proletariat is insufficiently prepared to unite the peasantry and seize power, is thereby incapable of bringing the democratic revolution to its conclusion. On the contrary, in a country where the proletariat has power in its hands as the result of the democratic revolution, the subsequent fate of the dictatorship and socialism is not only and not so much dependent in the final analysis upon the national productive forces, as it is upon the development of the international socialist revolution.

12. The theory of socialism in one country which rose on the yeast of the reaction against October is the only theory that consistently, and to the very end, opposes the theory of the permanent revolution.

The attempt of the epigones, under the blows of our criticism, to confine the application of the theory of socialism in one country exclusively to Russia, because of its specific characteristics (its extensiveness and its natural resources) does not improve matters but only makes them worse. The break with the international position always leads to a national messianism, that is, to attribute special prerogatives and peculiarities to one's own country, which would permit it to play a rôle that other countries cannot attain.

The world division of labor, the dependence of Soviet industry upon foreign technique, the dependence of the productive forces of the advanced countries of Europe upon Asiatic raw materials, etc., etc., make the construction of a socialist society in any single country impossible.

13. The theory of Stalin-Bucharin not only contrasts the democratic revolution quite mechanically to the socialist revolution, but also tears the national revolution from the international path.

This theory sets the revolution in the backward countries the task of establishing an unrealizable régime of the democratic dictatorship, it contrasts this régime to the dictatorship of the proletariat, thus introducing illusion and fiction into politics, paralyzing the struggle for power of the proletariat in the East, and hampering the victory of the colonial revolution.

The very seizure of power by the proletariat signifies, from the standpoint of the theory of the epigones, the completion of the revolution (to "nine-tenths", according to Stalin's formula) and the opening of the epoch of national reform.   The theory of the kulak growing into socialism and the theory of the "neutralization" of the world bourgeoisie are consequently inseparable from the theory of socialism in one country.   They stand and fall together.

By the theory of national socialism, the Communist International is degraded to a weapon useful only for the struggle against military intervention. The present policy of the Comintern, its régime, and the selection of its leading personnel, correspond entirely to the debasement of the Communist International to an auxiliary corps which is not destined to solve independent tasks.

14. The program of the Comintern created by Bucharin is thoroughly eclectic. It makes the hopeless attempt to reconcile the theory of socialism in one country with Marxian internationalism, which is, however, inseparable from the permanent character of the world revolution.   The struggle of the Communist Left Opposition for a correct policy and a healthy régime in the Communist International is inseparably combined with a struggle for a Marxian program. The question of the program in turn is inseparable from the question of the two mutually exclusive theories: the theory of permanent revolution and the theory of socialism in one country.   The problem of the permanent revolution has long ago outgrown the episodic differences of opinion between Lenin and Trotsky, which were completely exhausted by history.   The struggle is between the basic ideas of Marx and Lenin on the one side and the eclectics of the Centrists on the other.

CONSTANTINOPLE, *November 30, 1929*

CPSIA information can be obtained at www.ICGtesting.com
Printed in the USA
241294LV00002B/125/P